# THE REMOVALIST

# On the Front Line of Death Care

## Matthew Franklin Sias

Originally self-published by Matthew Franklin Sias in 2017

Published by Vulpine Press in the United Kingdom in 2019

ISBN 978-1-912701-40-7

Cover by Claire Wood

www.vulpine-press.com

For Klaire, a most welcome surprise.

# Introduction

Death and taxes are the only two inescapable realities of this earthly life. Both can be put off for years, but in the end, we've all got to pay the Tax Man as well as the Grim Reaper. Since I was never any good at doing anyone else's taxes, much less my own, I somehow fell into the business of working with the dead. I wasn't born into the business, as none of my family members held jobs even tangentially related to mortuary science or forensic medicine. How I popped out of the womb with such an interest in a field from which most people would sprint as fast as they could, I haven't a clue. At any rate, I've been at it a while, and have had the dubious privilege to be witness, hundreds of times, to what remains after a soul has taken leave of the physical.

My first book *Silent Siren: Memoirs of a Lifesaving Mortician* chronicled both my career in emergency medical services and my experiences in death care. The book spanned a period of over twenty years and attempted to meld my seemingly divergent experiences into a cohesive whole. Whether I was successful at this endeavor is up to the readers.

This book takes off where *Silent Siren* left off—not in terms of chronology, but as a more in-depth look at one man's experiences solely in the field of death care. My hope is that these short stories will make the reader consider his own mortality and what one would like to be remembered for long after one is gone from this earth. Furthermore, I hope to shed some light on the oft-misunderstood interval between the time a person's heart stops beating and the moment the last shovelful of dirt is tamped down on his grave.

Though I have tried not to make this book a gratuitous gore-fest, death and the changes a body goes through after the heart stops are not pleasant, so be warned. Those with a weak stomach may want to cover their eyes in places. But for those who don't shy away from the unabashed descriptions contained herein, I implore you to read on...

# Speed Kills

There is something profoundly gloomy about plucking chunks of rain-soaked brain from the grass, especially in the dark, and especially when those chunks are arrayed in a six-yard radius from a dead man's car.

My numb toes squish in sodden socks. Ten minutes into this call and I have already stepped into a muddy morass inconveniently located between my van and what remains of a car so mangled I can't even tell if it's an SUV or sedan.

Well, that and my camera won't work properly. What with the rain and the pitch-darkness, the lens won't focus on anything, so I have to resort to aiming my anemic flashlight beam at an object to get a focus. It sort of works, and sort of doesn't.

The beam of the flashlight strikes fractured CDs, glass shards, beer cans...and brain tissue. I walk with my red plastic bag and throw the bigger chunks in. If I've left any smaller bits, the birds will eat them in the morning. The circle of life. The fire siren mounted to a nearby station howls, hailing volunteers to another call being dispatched. It's haunting. Rain pounds.

The accident scene is a study in centrifugal force. After careening out of control, the car flipped end over end multiple times, flinging bits of itself—and its luckless passenger—yards away.

The State Patrol detective had surmised that the driver had not been wearing his seat belt, and, as the car flipped, the single driver had pin-balled around the interior until the windows shattered and his head was exposed to the exterior. With a couple of more flips, the contents of his cranium had been flung in an arc pattern spanning several yards.

The rear bumper, bearing the license plate, is in the street. I take note of the number for my report. The car is in a grassy right-of-way next to several homes. The lights are on in the homes and a few onlookers have gathered to observe the results of the mayhem.

The Patrol sergeant points out a middle-aged man standing near the patrol cars, holding an umbrella. "He's a neighbor. Thinks he may know where this guy lives."

I introduce myself and attempt to scribble his name on my damp report form before realizing that pens don't write in the rain. Pencils do, but I don't have one with me.

"Terrible driver," says the man. "Used to drive like a bat out of hell through here every day. Kids and pets in this neighborhood. I figured something would happen eventually."

And happen it did. The trail of debris is nearly a half-block long.

"He lives in the marina," says the man. "He and some kid. Maybe his son."

I thank him for his time and finally turn my attention to the largest chunk of the car and its mortal contents.

Squished in the passenger's seat, dressed in a leather jacket and jeans, is what is left of Randy Moore, age fifty-three, according to his driver's license. The top of his head is gone, fractured skull gaping like the cracked shell of a crab, contents evacuated, pink flaps of hairy scalp splayed to the sides. One eyeball, still tethered by an optic nerve, lolls onto Randy's cheek. The other is pushed deeply into the socket. Absurdly, his right index finger points at the dash, at the speedometer to be exact, as though he were indicating the speed at which he was traveling. The speedometer is pegged at eighty miles per hour.

The removal from the vehicle is fairly straightforward. I'm able to pry open the passenger door pretty easily. A police officer holds it open for me as I yank Randy's remains out and slide them onto the rain-slick plastic liner that lies on the gurney. It's an indelicate process at best, with nowhere near the care afforded to the living, but Randy isn't around to experience it. I slide a pant leg up to attach an ID tag. Instead of flesh, I am greeted by titanium—an artificial leg. Perhaps as the result of a previous car accident?

I load Randy into the van as police strobe lights reflect off the pounding raindrops, and then make my way back to the morgue, where under more controlled and better lit conditions, I take additional photographs and measurements of the body.

As with most any case, notification of the next of kin is by far the worst part. I sift through the multitude of dilapidated and dog-eared cards in the man's wallet until I come upon a business card for A.D. Moore Construction.

I make the assumption that A.D. Moore is a relative and dial the number.

It seems to come as no surprise to the elderly Mr. Moore that his son has died. He'd had his brushes with the law, with alcohol, and with excessive speed. Wearily, almost resignedly, he hands the phone to his other son, Randy's brother.

The son explains that Randy had moved out west for the winter from Wisconsin to be with his son, who lived on a boat. It was too cold for Randy in Wisconsin, so he chose here, which seemed odd. I gaze out the rain-streaked office window. Wouldn't southern California be a better choice?

How can I get a hold of Randy's son in Washington so he can claim Randy's personal effects?

I can't. He's a fugitive from the law with warrants out of Wisconsin and is going to make himself as scarce as possible.

I tell the other son to make arrangements with a funeral home in

Washington State and I will transfer Randy's personal effects there to be sent back to Wisconsin to his family.

Since Randy is the sole occupant of the vehicle and his injuries are obvious, I decide against arranging an autopsy. The cause of death is obvious, the manner—accidental—not quite so obvious, and there is nobody to prosecute but the dead man.

In lieu of a full autopsy, I draw samples of blood and urine for toxicology analysis. Families often want to know the state of mind of a person who dies due to accident or potential suicide and whether or not his judgment had been clouded by drugs or alcohol.

Drawing a urine sample is fairly straightforward and involves simply plunging a needle into the general area of the bladder, pulling back the plunger, and hoping something yellowish comes back. It is a reliable test for drugs and alcohol, and is preferred over blood.

Obtaining a central blood sample is a bit trickier. I prefer the sub-clavian approach, in which I insert a very long needle underneath the collarbone at a fifteen-degree angle and hope to get blood. I am usually successful at this, but sometimes have to resort to jabbing a needle directly into the heart. There is nothing delicate about death investigation.

With any luck, the toxicology results will be available in about six weeks. The state lab will send us an analysis of any alcohol, narcotics, or methamphetamines they had found in our samples. Due, in part, to the "CSI effect" families expect the results much sooner and often call every week or so until they are given resolution.

Tired, damp, muddy, and a little bloody, I drive the Big Green Death Wagon back to my home, where my little dog, all five pounds of fluff and unbridled enthusiasm, greets me. He knows not where I've been, or even how long I've been gone. All he knows is that his "daddy" is home. That and I smell much more interesting than usual.

Rejuvenated by the scalding hot water of a shower, I crawl into bed next to my sleeping wife. The pager is silent, for now.

# Pet Cemetery

I was a weird child, precocious but disturbingly so, with a seemingly inborn awareness of the prevalence of sickness and death. As my great-aunt sat in a haze of cigarette smoke, I had very soberly advised her, "Aunt Clarice, the Surgeon General has determined that cigarette smoking is dangerous to your health." I was perhaps five at the time.

"Well," she had hacked, "you just tell the Surgeon General that I smoke low-tar."

Aunt Clarice died several years later of lung cancer. As she was lying in her hospital bed, breathing her last, she had apparently asked her doctor, tongue in cheek, "Do you think the cigarettes had anything to do with this?" She never lost her sense of humor.

I was a bit of a loner, preferring the company of animals to that of humans. They seemed to understand me and were non-judgmental. So my childhood was spent in the company of my cat, Custard, more dog-like than any cat I had ever met, who would run to the end of the driveway to greet me as I got off the school bus in the afternoon.

Even at ten years old, I seemed destined for a future in death care. Much to my mother's vexation, I designated a small section of her vegetable garden as an animal cemetery. I would find a robin that had struck the window and perished, wipe the blood from her beak, and place her in a shoebox with a paper towel pulled up to her breast. For some reason, I thought that putting cotton in the eyes was a good idea. A splash of Mother's perfume to mask the odor of early decomposition, and the robin was ready for an open-casket viewing.

My experimentation with cremation didn't go so well. I had found a mole that my cat had mauled to death, and attempted to ignite it, using Vaseline and toilet paper as fuel. I managed only to produce a mole roast that even my cat found unpalatable. Mr. Mole was then buried after a simple, closed-casket ceremony.

I would often hold graveside services and read from the Episcopal prayer book *Burial of the Dead, Rite I.* Not surprisingly, I was the sole attendee at these graveside services, which often concluded with the placement of a small wooden cross atop the mound of dirt.

My family's reaction to my amateur mortuary business was one of dismay. While my younger brother busied himself with taking engines apart and putting them back together again in the wrong order, I was quite content to fertilize my mother's zucchinis with the victims of beak versus window accidents and homicides committed by the cat. When my grandmother came to visit, I invited her for a tour of the cemetery. She had politely declined.

For larger animals, I had constructed a pole stretcher consisting of on old sheet stretched between two pieces of wood, tacked together with staples. The only problem was, there was nobody to hold the other end of the stretcher. Nonetheless, I scooped a few rotting raccoon carcasses off the road near our house and buried them as well. It seemed my duty to play neighborhood animal mortician.

I fancied myself an amateur pathologist at times and attempting to do postmortem examinations on a variety of small deceased creatures, among them a mouse and a salamander. Unfortunately, I was not very talented at this, and my instruments—safety scissors and a dull scalpel I obtained from a child's microscope kit—left much to be desired. Birds were especially difficult, what with the feathers and all. My talents certainly did not lend themselves to hunting or anything involving fine muscle coordination.

On rare occasions, I felt compelled to study the decomposition process. I exhumed the bodies of a bird or two, always finding them in a malodorous state of advanced decay. My neighbor, six years old or so at the time, watched me bury, dig up, and re-bury my clients and, given his young age, mistakenly believed that I was planting bird trees. He would come over every so often to see if the "bird tree" seedlings had sprouted yet.

# From EMT to DOA

I've been in the "death business" for about ten years, in two capacities; as a funeral home removal technician and as a death investigator. While the former simply involved transport to a mortuary for ultimate disposal, the latter was a bit more involved, allowing me to use my sleuthing abilities to arrive at a cause and manner of death. Sometimes this involved an autopsy, but more often it required simply the ability to determine, from examination of the body and evaluation of medical records, a probable reason for the person's death.

In both capacities, I was a transporter, a "removalist" as I'd like to say, one whose job it was to get the dead from whichever odd predicament they happened to get themselves into, to their destination, be it a funeral home, crematory, or county morgue.

I've removed bodies from, among other places, beds, bathtubs, backyards, back alleys, rivers, mountains, cars, boats, lofts, cruise ships, planes, and once, from within a hollowed-out tree stump. The bodies have been in various states of decay and mutilation, from a woman still warm after a fatal heart attack, to a man found dead in a sunken car after six months. Each situation has presented its own logistical challenges and occupational hazards. At times I have wondered if this is the last body my aching back can handle.

The removal is perhaps the aspect of the death business that is least appreciated by the general public. In earlier times, when a death would occur at home, a funeral director would typically respond and help lay out the body for viewing in a home. An undertaker was first a cabinet maker, who fashioned coffins himself, and next a person who would "undertake" the task of preparing the body and burying it. Death was a community event, often with the presence of a horse-drawn or motorized hearse arriving at the residence. Many black communities still expect the formality and tradition of yesteryear, and black-owned funeral homes will still respond to home deaths with a hearse, the director dressed to the nines.

For most in the United States at large, with the exception of the Deep South, cremation has achieved a stronghold. In contrast with tradition, Grandma is made to disappear quietly out the back door and into an unmarked van, only to appear again days later as a container of cremated remains.

The basic qualifications of a removal technician are that he or she needs to have a driver's license, a strong back, a strong stomach, and, probably most importantly, the decorum to know what to say or what not to say to the loved ones of a deceased person. Since the "first call" as it is known, is the initial contact a funeral home has with a family, the way a removal is carried out can make or break the reputation of that mortuary. It's a simple job, but one that has to be done right. There are no second chances.

Depending on the area, removal personnel may be unlicensed technicians or licensed funeral director/embalmers, coroner's technicians, or board-certified death investigators. As society slowly shifts away from traditional burial to cremation, there will be less need for embalmers, but there will always be a need for caring, compassionate people willing to get up at four in the morning and drive to a residence where Grandpa has passed away in his sleep.

Removal technicians are an anonymous lot. The funeral director, whose public persona puts him at the forefront of a congregation, conducting death's symphony, is a familiar sight. The highly educated, albeit often bizarre forensic pathologist, whose highly specialized skills and knowledge may put him in the middle of a high-profile murder case, is well known to the public, popularized in such TV shows as *Crossing Jordan* and *Quincy, M.E.* The lowly removal tech is akin to a stagehand, dressed in black, who moves set pieces between acts of a play, largely unseen, doing work that is, while necessary, certainly inglorious and thankless. Yet we were out there, at all hours of the day and night, in the rain and snow, in the most austere of circumstances.

Our equipment is basic. The vans we use to perform our work resemble stripped-down ambulances. Like an ambulance gurney, our cots are wheeled, have multiple positions, and are designed to fit through narrow hallways and doorways. The difference lies in the comfort level. Mortuary cots have no pillows. The mattresses are thin, if they exist at all. A medical examiner's office where I once worked used three sheets, the first to wrap the body in, the second to cover the body, and the third, a "head soaker," an absorbent blanket to wrap around the heads of those with severe trauma, thus preventing blood from spilling all over the floorboards of the van. Like an emergency vehicle, our dashboards are crammed with map books, GPS units, communications equipment, and sometimes the consoles for flashing lights and sirens. There are no stethoscopes, no bandages. Only boxes of rubber gloves, body bags, and toe tags. We are the EMTs of the dead.

I came to work with the dead in a roundabout way. I was an emergency medical technician with my local fire department, and often crossed paths with funeral directors or deputy coroners when our attempts at resuscitation had been in vain. I discovered I had a knack for speaking to people who had just lost a loved one. I became skilled at what I would later come to know as "funeral speak," the relatively monotone speech pattern characterized by euphemisms cleverly designed to soften the blow of death. A person hadn't died, he'd passed. It wasn't a corpse, it was remains.

As the years passed in my work as an emergency medical technician, and later as a paramedic, I became increasingly frustrated with the shift in our clientele from those who were deathly ill and needed urgent intervention, to those that chose to use our mobile intensive care units as expensive taxi cabs. Thirty years ago, few people would think to call 911 if they had experienced flu-like symptoms for a week. Sure, there were a few folks, even then, who struggled with the concept of what constituted an emergency (and struggled with life in general, for that matter). But the 911 "system" had become a victim of its own success. Ingrained in the public consciousness was now the notion that if anything went awry, from an infected toenail to an airline disaster, one must summon the cavalry in the form of men and women in crisp blue uniforms, arriving with great fanfare, in a blaze of multicolored lights. In this modern world of instant gratification, "toughing it out" seemed to be a lost art. It was as though people expected to feel good all the time, and if they didn't, something must be done. Somebody must be responsible.

I saw the changes in society as a whole reflected in an attitude towards laziness, learned helplessness, and instant gratification. Many times a week I would respond to a report of a "slumper"—somebody pulled over to the side of the road, leaned over or appearing unresponsive. A passerby, not wishing to be bothered with actually checking on the person's welfare, would call 911 and set into motion a fire engine, an ambulance, the local police, and possibly other authorities, who would rush, lights and sirens to the scene and invariably find the "patient" taking a cat-nap, reading a map, changing a tire, or engaged in extra-curricular activity with a friend.

With the advent of text messaging and smart phones, the art of conversation was being lost, replaced by terse, often ungrammatical sound bites. Online news articles became truncated to a single paragraph. Sitcoms solved massive problems in the course of half an hour.

Forensic dramas proliferated, misrepresenting the tedious and labor-intensive world of applied science and replacing it with a non-stop series of brilliant insight, clear-cut, black-and-white answers, and the near-instantaneous return of lab tests, which in reality, take weeks if not longer. Entertainment seemed to become more and more banal. One could become famous for really no reason at all. Perhaps our rising star is a gay dwarf who bids on abandoned storage lockers. Within months he has his own show and becomes more famous than Elvis. Talent be damned. Hard work? Unnecessary.

And so it was with emergency medical services, a microcosm of a populace that craves instant results and feel-good medicine. Welcome to our Emergency Room and Psychotherapy Department! Shorter waits than those guys across town! Leave your dignity and common sense at the door!

While certainly my job as a paramedic involved its share of legitimate calls for help, much of it seemed to be so much whining. When a person is able to call 911 and then lumber about his or her apartment, gathering shoes, clothes, cigarettes, and a cell phone, he or she damn well has enough energy to take a taxi to the hospital, or, better yet, an urgent care clinic. I had heard more times than I care to recall, "I don't have the money for a taxi." When I pointed out that a $15 taxi ride is a hell of a lot less expensive than a $700 ride in a mobile intensive care unit, I was often met with the response "But I have coupons." Since we couldn't legally refuse transport, we simply wheeled or walked these decision-impaired folks out of their malodorous hovels, past their seventy-inch TVs, and shipped them off to the ER to be evaluated by overworked ER physicians who would sigh, dip their urine, and boot them out the door with a prescription for Cipro. Sometimes the bill was paid by the state. Often it was written off.

For all the time I've spent providing a taxi service to those with poor decision-making skills, I have spent easily twice as much time ferrying nursing home patients to and from the emergency department. It seems that nobody is allowed to die anymore. Those who are clearly moribund are perpetually sent to the ER in the vain hope that something can be done to interrupt their natural and inevitable slide into total body failure. So when ninety-eight-year-old Maude won't wake up and has no blood pressure, we MUST ship her off to the ER in the hopes that she will recover enough to go back to work as a lion tamer and live to be one hundred and twenty. But what kind of a life are we really bringing her back to? Another, perhaps more painful illness or mishap that will finally take her life in a matter of weeks or months? It got disheartening.

So, after a long and illustrious career in the business of taking care of sick people, I took a much-needed hiatus from the care of those with warm blood still flowing through their veins and opted for more quiet customers. There were advantages, to be sure. My dead customers never swore or spat at me, never whined or demanded pain medications, and were generally much more agreeable than the living. On the other hand, though, the dead completely refuse to stand up and sit on the stretcher, and are a little leakier than their living counterparts—but not much.

In contrast to my work as a medic, my vocation as a death worker brought to the surface a sort of compassion in me that I was sure had long ago gone the way of the Dodo. It was hard not to feel sad for those who had lost a loved one, even if that loved one had led a derelict or unsavory life. Even if a family had long ago lost hope, at some point, these silent clients were loved, had hopes, dreams, and aspirations. Those inert and insensate bags of protoplasm had once been animated with the soul of a brother, sister, father, mother, aunt, or uncle.

I worked for a short time as a death investigator in a major metropolitan area before transitioning to a mortuary service just south of there, in the same county. I generally enjoyed the work of a death investigator, though the transition from emergency medical services to death care was a bit abrupt, and I wasn't as focused as I should have been.

There was still a part of me that wanted to continue in EMS, so for a time I continued to work as a paramedic and took a part-time job as a removal tech at a funeral home that represented other funeral homes.

The mortuary service couldn't be found in the phone book, and our business was located in a large warehouse which housed two gigantic walk-in refrigeration units, an embalming room, and three roaring crematory retorts. We did the work that other funeral homes didn't have the time, the facilities, or the inclination to do. In our gray, unmarked minivans, we would be called at all hours of the day and night to pick up bodies and transport them either back to our facility, or to the client funeral homes.

The death call would come in, and we would travel, to a home usually, and identify ourselves to the family: "I am Matt and this is so-and-so, representing Apex Funeral Home." This was especially odd when I, a white man, was called to represent a black-owned funeral home. The family usually caught on pretty quickly that I was a vendor, instead of an actual funeral home employee. Families would ask us questions specific to the funeral home, and we would have to tell them, "The funeral director will answer all of your questions on Monday."

Simple paperwork was involved. We obtained name, address, date of birth, time of death, and we documented any clothing or valuables on the body. On a house call, we would attach an ankle tag to the body, wrap the remains in plastic, zip them up in a bag, and wheel the body to the van. Simple stuff.

At the client funeral home, the procedure was pretty simple: log the body into "The Book of Death" and place it on a shelf in the cooler. A couple of homes wanted us to elevate the head on a block, to prevent engorgement of the facial features and inconvenient "drainage," and to paint an anti-dehydration cream onto the face, in case there was a viewing.

Few people realize that a good percentage of the anonymous

minivans zooming past them on the freeway are actually removal vehicles. If the driver of a minivan is wearing a suit and tie, chances are good that he is hauling a silent customer or two. The dead are closer than we think.

# Driving the Death Wagon

A light but dreary drizzle spatters the windshield of the gold Chevy Astro van as I make a right turn out of the mortuary toward the freeway. My companion is Mr. Anthony Trevino, who reclines silently on the mortuary gurney in the back, zipped up snugly in a maroon pouch, oblivious to the weather or anything else for that matter. Embalmed and dressed in a yellow moisture-proof garment known as a Unionall, he is on his way to a Seattle funeral home to await his viewing and funeral service. Unlike some of the other bodies I transport, his needs to be handled with the utmost care, since he is destined not for cremation, but for burial. A half-drunk cup of coffee sits in the cup holder, lukewarm from sitting in the van as I had gathered paperwork.

I approach the first intersection, a block away from the mortuary. I slow briefly for the red light and then, as the light turns green, accelerate through. Just to the edge of my peripheral vision, I catch a green blur approaching at high speed. Then, before I can take any evasive action, I feel the impact on the passenger's side. The van spins 180 degrees and comes to a screeching halt on the other side of the intersection, facing the direction from whence it came.

I step out of the van and survey the damage. An older model sedan is stopped in the middle of the intersection, its hood caved in, steam rising from the fractured radiator. Glass from a broken headlight gleams in the rain. The left headlight, more or less intact, points absurdly towards the sky amid crumpled metal. Tentatively, the driver exits, followed by three short Hispanic men, who appear unfazed by the event.

"Is everybody okay?" I ask.

"Yeah, we're fine. I dinnit see you coming," the driver says. "Sorry, man."

Another car approaches. The driver flips on his hazards, gets out, and begins to direct traffic around the wrecked vehicle. The intersection is completely blocked. I make my way around to the passenger's side of the van where the impact occurred, in order to survey the damage. The sliding door is caved in and inoperable. I cup my hands to peer through the tinted side windows and notice that the gurney has slid all the way to the right and upended itself, its wheels pointed towards the ceiling, like a beetle flipped on its back.

The men mill around on the sidewalk, seemingly unsure of what to do next.

"I guess we should exchange insurance information," I say wearily.

The driver pipes up, "I don't know, man. This is my cousin's car."

I take my cell phone out of my pocket and dial 911 for the police to come and take a report. Then I dial the number for Jerry, the mortuary owner. He says he will respond to the scene shortly. As I wait for them to arrive, the rain dumps.

"Hey, can I borrow your phone, man?" says the driver. "I gotta call my cousin."

With irritation, I hand him my phone and he proceeds to monopolize it for the next ten minutes. Later, I will curse myself for letting him use it. *He's just hit my van in a car that isn't even his, doesn't appear to have insurance, and now he wants to borrow my phone?*

A police car arrives, lights whirling, and blocks off the intersection. The officer interviews the driver of the car before speaking with me.

"The guy has no license and no insurance," he says. "This your van?"

"No. It's a company van."

"What company?"

"It's a mortuary van."

The police officer smirks. "You got a body in there?"

"Yes, I do."

Jerry shows up in his pickup and I explain the circumstances. He asks me if I'm okay then turns his attention to the damaged van.

He opens up the back doors to reveal the upended gurney.

"Where were you transporting to?" he asks.

"Evergreen-Washelli."

"Let's get this thing right-side-up again."

I climb up into the van, taking one end, and Jerry stays outside on the other end. We flip the gurney and its oblivious cargo back over again. Mr. Trevino has just been in a postmortem car accident, and he didn't realize it. Even if he did, he probably wouldn't care.

I unzip the cot cover and partially open the bag. Mr. Trevino doesn't look bad, though his nose is a little more askew than I remember it being.

"You know what would make the other driver really feel bad?" Jerry says, a broad grin beginning to creep across his face.

"What?"

"Put the dead guy in the front seat and say it was a fatality."

# The Death Business

On those rare occasions when I take time off for leisure and associate with "normal" people, I sometimes am asked about my work and the role I play in the Business of Death. Coroners and funeral directors are but two of the more well-known players in a rather more complex co-operation of individuals whose job it is to get the dead to their final destination.

Depending on local protocol, resources, and customs, when a dead body is discovered, it may put into motion a response involving police officers, paramedics, hospice nurses, coroner and/or medical examiner personnel, removal technicians, pathologists, embalmers, crematory operators, funeral directors, clergy of all conceivable faiths, gravediggers, and various bureaucratic offices such as the County Health Department and Social Security Office.

So, let's consider the fate of one such dead person, the entirely fictional ex-taxpayer Mary Jones, aged sixty-two years, whose brother finds her dead in her apartment one fine summer day.

Mary's brother hasn't heard from her in three days, and after calling her home phone, cell phone, and attempting to message her on Facebook, he decides to pay a visit. Finding the door unlocked, he enters and notices a faint odor that, from a year he spent driving a rendering truck, he recognizes as decomposition. After finding Mary facedown in the bathroom, he calls 911.

County paramedics arrive first, and after a cursory examination, declare her dead. Because she has signs of early decomposition, they choose not to slap EKG electrodes—or "fairy stickers" as they are sometimes derisively known—to confirm the inevitable, represented by a very straight line running across the EKG screen. On the heels of the paramedics comes a sheriff's deputy, required to respond to all cases of "unattended deaths."

The paramedics clear the scene within minutes, leaving the deputy to ascertain any obvious signs of foul play. Though Mary's door was found unlocked, there are no signs of forcible entry, no blood spatters streaked along the walls, no knife sticking out of her back. He finds three medication bottles, which her brother thinks are for her high blood pressure and diabetes. If the deputy were to note any examples of foul play, his next call would likely be either to his sergeant or the on-duty detective, either or both of whom would respond to the scene and conduct further investigation, sometimes lasting many hours until the body is removed.

Since there are no obvious signs of foul play, the deputy calls dispatch and requests the County Coroner respond. If the death were considered suspicious, the coroner might respond with detectives or be asked to wait until a preliminary on-scene investigation had been completed. It all depends on local protocol.

The deputy is not allowed to touch or move the body until the coroner arrives, except in exigent circumstances, such as the need to establish identification. State laws designate law enforcement as being "in charge of the scene" while coroner personnel are considered to be "in charge of the body."

Since Mary's death occurs in a relatively small county, a coroner system is in place. A coroner is an elected official charged with determining the cause and manner of death. The coroner is usually not a medical doctor (but can be) and there are few qualifications for his office other than to be a resident of the county and have no felony convictions. Many elected coroners are funeral home owners, retired police officers, or paramedics. Experience counts, but there is currently no formal education required. A coroner can employ one or more deputies to act on his or her behalf, and usually contracts with a pathologist to perform autopsies when needed.

If Mary had lived in a larger county, her death would be handled by a medical examiner's office. The chief of such an office is a medical doctor, usually a board-certified forensic pathologist, whose job it is also to determine the cause and manner of death. The Chief Medical Examiner may also employ other pathologists as well as medico-legal death investigators—the equivalent of deputy coroners, to assist in these endeavors. Whether a county uses a coroner system or a medical examiner system comes down to cost and population. Most small counties cannot afford full-time forensic pathologists, who may command upwards of $200,000 a year.

The coroner arrives and begins his scene investigation, beginning with interviewing both the deputy and Mary's brother to determine the circumstances of the death. When did Mary's brother last speak to her and did she seem to be in her usual state of health at that time? Did she have any health problems? Who was her doctor and did the brother know when she might have last seen that doctor?

Next, the coroner photographs the scene, beginning with "the big picture," photos of the rooms of the house, including the bathroom and kitchen, the position of the body from several different angles, the toilet, the refrigerator, and possibly even the ceiling. A seemingly pointless photograph could lend valuable evidence to a case when it is reviewed later in light of new information. It is easy to focus first on the body, and in the process, miss valuable clues from the surroundings.

After photographing the scene, the coroner turns his attention to the body. The nightgown Mary is wearing, as well as her necklace and rings, are carefully documented, in photographic and written form. As well as speaking for the dead, death investigators have an obligation to safeguard their belongings and return them to the next of kin.

With the assistance of the deputy sheriff, the coroner turns Mary onto her back and continues his examination. Mary has a greenish discoloration of her lower abdomen, as well as dark, bloody fluid exuding from her mouth, both signs of early decomposition. The coroner manipulates her limbs to ascertain the degree of rigor mortis, or stiffening of the body. Her rigor is described as "easily breakable" since decomposition has caused rigor mortis to fade. The anterior or front surface of her body is stained maroon, owing to her blood settling due to gravity, the phenomenon known as postmortem lividity. Lividity that is not consistent with the position the body was found in is often a tell-tale sign that the body has been moved. For example, if she was to be found facedown, but the lividity was evident on her back, she would have been moved after her death. In Mary's case, her lividity is considered fixed; it does not blanch to light pressure, indicating that she had been dead at least ten hours.

Further examination of the body includes checking for petechiae—pinpoint hemorrhages visible in the inner membranes of the eye—sometimes (but not always) an indication of strangulation. Her head is felt for obvious fractures and her clothing is moved to check for obvious injuries.

Since Mary has medical history—diabetes and high blood pressure—and is of an age when death is not necessarily expected, but not out of the ordinary, considering her medical history, the coroner is coming close to reaching a conclusion that Mary died naturally, as a result of the devastating long-term effects of her disease processes.

But there is a problem. In the wastebasket to the left of Mary's head, the coroner discovers two empty medication bottles, both labeled Hydrocodone, one prescribed a month prior and the other prescribed three days prior. There was no way Mary could have been taking the medication as prescribed. The empty pill bottles cast doubt on the coroner's previous assessment that the death was natural. Was it suicidal? Was it accidental? No suicide note is found, though Mary's brother said she had been depressed lately. The coroner decides to have an autopsy performed after a consultation with Mary's personal doctor.

The time has come for Mary's body to be removed from the residence and taken to a location where she will have an autopsy performed.

Since the County Coroner has relatively few cases per month and thus no pressing need for his own transporting vehicle, he relies on the services of several funeral homes in the area that have contracts to perform removals.

In about twenty minutes, a silver van pulls up to the curb. It's subtle and unmarked with the exception of the telltale curved Landau panels covering the rear windows, indicating that it is a mortuary vehicle. A man and woman in dark suits step out, the woman carrying a clipboard.

The woman introduces herself as a funeral director and expresses her condolences to Mary's brother before speaking to the police officer and coroner. Meanwhile, the man, a removal technician, silently surveys the scene, his experienced eye noting obstacles, the presence or absence of stairs, and the size of the hallway before viewing the body.

As the funeral director writes down information given to her by the deputy and coroner, the technician snaps an identification bracelet on Mary's ankle with her name, case number, and date. To mix up bodies is very embarrassing.

Since there are no stairs, the removal crew can wheel their cot directly into the apartment. However, getting Mary from where she is in the bathroom to the cot is a somewhat more complicated affair. The cot will not fit into the bathroom, much less the narrow hallway that leads to it. The cot, a narrow bed with collapsible legs, is lowered to the ground inside the living room, the zippered shroud is opened, and two seatbelt-style straps are unbuckled and extended.

The removal technician brings a zippered canvas bag known as a disaster pouch, the politically correct term for a body bag, to where Mary lies. Why this is the preferred term, I will never know, as it seems that disasters are things generally to be avoided.

The crew rolls Mary to her side and she emits a groan, startling her brother, but not fazing the removal crew in the least. The groan is caused by residual air escaping her lungs and passing through her vocal cords. After being zipped into the disaster pouch, she is slid along the floor to the waiting cot. Such a maneuver may seem indelicate, however, since Mary weighs north of two hundred pounds, but it is saving the backs, and thus the careers, of our two mortuary folks.

The crew places Mary on the cot, straps her in, zips the shroud, and lifts the cot into the upright position. They wheel her to the van and load her in the back, the wheels collapsing and sliding in at the pull of a lever.

Mary's body is brought to the funeral home where the autopsy is performed. The practice of conducting autopsies at funeral homes is quite common, especially in small communities. In fact, the popular image of an autopsy suite as a vast, sterile sea of stainless steel tables, glowing computer screens, and dim lighting is by far the exception. Many autopsies are still performed in the bowels of hospitals, the basements of old houses, and even in retrofitted barns. If the dead could vote, they may opt to fund the CSI version, but unfortunately, in our death-denying society, they don't.

The following morning her autopsy will be performed by a contract pathologist, akin to a "rent-a-doctor" who also serves three other counties and carries his supplies around with him in a 1995 Nissan Pathfinder.

Later that afternoon, Mary's brother meets with a funeral director to discuss "disposition" as it is known—the choices of burial, cremation, shipping out of state, or donation for medical research. As luck would have it, Mary already had a "pre-need" contract signed with the funeral home, indicating that she would prefer to be buried, following a traditional Catholic recitation of the Rosary and funeral service. Since Mary has already made her own arrangements, she has signed her own embalming authorization, chosen the music she would like played, and specified the clothing she is to wear in her casket.

# Hospital Removals

Nowhere is the specter of death more unwelcome than in a hospital. In an institution seemingly bent on preserving life, no matter what the cost, hospitals seem to treat the logical end of life as a failure or even as an embarrassment. While the ER and main entrances are emblazoned with neon signs and decorated with carefully sculpted shrubbery, the morgue is banished to the rear of the hospital or to some obscure, unmarked side entrance, flanked by dumpsters and full biohazard bins. If the ER entrance is a toothy grin, welcoming all comers, the morgue is the asshole, grudgingly jettisoning the effluvium of failure.

A hospital removal is a pretty simple affair. Unless the body is very large, only one person is dispatched from the funeral home. The technician arrives, backs up to the loading dock, and then enters with the empty cot. A security guard usually meets the technician, points out the correct body, and directs him or her to sign the necessary paperwork. Security is generally not thrilled with this aspect of their duties. Many a security guard I have met has stood in the corner, arms folded, and scowled at me as though I am some sort of hunchbacked ghoul. If I try to make small talk or crack a joke, the security guard usually responds with a weak smile and a mumble.

Usually I unzip the bag and check the ID tag on the body as well as its general condition. The funeral director usually wants to know if the body is viewable as is or if further preparation is required. Patients who have been in an intensive care unit for weeks are often waterlogged and swollen, necessitating special embalming treatment. The bodies all wear the uniform of the deceased—hospital gown with an incontinent pad under the derriere. Besides the variation in size, they pretty much all look the same: pale, mouth agape, and eyes half-closed.

The dead are not received from the morgue into shiny black hearses, but instead into unmarked, inauspicious minivans in all manner of dull colors. From there, they are made to disappear, perhaps to warehouses full of humming refrigeration units and roaring crematory retorts, to be consumed by flames, only to reappear again as breadbox-sized urns, labeled in simple block letters with the dead person's name, years of life, and the name of the funeral home that directed the cremation. Or perhaps they are to be encased in oak or semi-precious metal caskets and consumed by the earth, their headstones the only visible reminder of their past existence.

Nowhere is this societal disconnection from death more evident than in the strange conveyances used to transport the newly deceased from the hospital bed to the refrigerator where they will chill for a while until claimed. The hospital trolley is, perhaps, emblematic of a death-denying society. It resembles any wheeled hospital bed, with two exceptions: the mattress is replaced by a cold steel tray, and a rectangular frame fits over the top, covered by a thick white canvas. The purpose of this frame is to completely obscure the shape of the body, so that when it is being wheeled down the hallway, nobody will be able to make out a head-like or tummy-like lump that would belie the trolley's purpose. It may as well be the dinner cart.

The trolley and its cumbersome lid are the bane of my existence in the morgue. I am thankful we don't have security cameras in our facility, as I would be caught swearing and fumbling around with the lid, attempting to get it to sit properly on the trolley without one end sliding off and banging onto the floor. And for what purpose? Patients and their families must know that death often occurs in a hospital. It has to happen *somewhere*. However, the physical representation of that death, the body itself, shrouded though it may be with sheets or in a bag, is banished from our awareness.

It is a relative rarity for a funeral director to make a removal directly from the hospital floor, and it seems only to be done when the cooler is full. When a man wearing a suit wheels a patient covered head to toe by a burgundy shroud, it is beyond obvious that the patient is not at all well. As I've wheeled my cargo into elevators or down a hallway, I'm given a wide berth by all I pass. Gazes are averted, nobody smiles or says hello. It's as close as I will probably ever come to being invisible, barely human, Charon on the river Styx, ferrying the dead to Hades.

# Morbid Questions

For those with a morbid curiosity, which I'm going to venture to guess is all of you, I'll answer a few of the more commonly asked questions of those of us odd enough to get into (and stay in) this business. The first of which is, "Why the hell would you do this job?"

Most children are asked at some point what they would like to be when they grow up and they usually respond with doctor, astronaut, firefighter, ballet dancer, cowboy, or some other heroic occupation. Never have I heard of a child saying, "I want to pick up dead bodies for a living!" For that matter, I've never heard of a child who aspires to be a HVAC repairman or a software engineer, but in our death-denying society, those responses might be met with a smile and an exclamation along the lines of, "Oh what a precocious child!" A child who announces he wants to be an undertaker might be met with muted horror on the part of the parents, a tight-lipped smile and an, "Oh, that's nice."

I must admit I was one of those morbid little children and faced ostracism for it in my younger years. Nobody wants to hear a child's detailed description of the embalming process over dinner, least of all my parents. Nevertheless, I felt an inexplicable calling to the death care field from an early age, and haven't let the squeamishness of others dampen my interest in all things thanatological.

Other than my inexplicable fascination with all things dead and decaying, obvious from an early age, my desire to work in the dismal trade stems from a desire to witness a part of life normally hidden from view, to be a member of an almost secret club of morticians, coroners, and pathologists, a club in which the initiates are bonded by their un-flappable ability to carry about their macabre business among the murdered, the decomposed, the vacant husks of former humans. To be able to thrive in a field most are terrified of is a source of pride for me. To be in the presence of those who have crossed over the great divide is oddly meaningful, in an ultimate sense.

Another question I am asked from time to time is, "How do you handle the smell?"

Your trusty flat-screen television brings you the gory spectacle of bloodied corpses on such popular shows as CSI and NCIS. Thus far, though, the technology does not exist to blast you with the vulture-gagging stench of a body marinating in a river for three months or the nauseating odor of an old alcoholic facedown in a puddle of vomit.

I had smelled a decomposing body before I came to work as a death investigator, but only at a respectful distance. As an emergency medical technician, I had pulled back the curtain of an old bread truck where an old man had been quietly decomposing in the summer heat for a week, took one belly-turning breath, and backed the hell out. Death confirmed. No further need for my presence. When I became an investigator, I no longer had the luxury of getting the hell out of Dodge. Decomps were our bread and butter. We had to examine them for injuries, turn them, rifle through their pockets for valuables, and even perform autopsies on their foul flesh.

In the first week of my employment as an investigator, I had asked another employee how she dealt with the smell. I was expecting an answer such as, "We use paper masks smeared with Vick's Vap-O-Rub or canister respirators and a cigar and tons of those little tree air fresheners." Instead she had replied, "We just gag and deal with it."

The smell is overwhelming at first but is quickly attenuated by the body's own defense system, the phenomenon known as olfactory fatigue. The longer we are continually exposed to the stink, the more bearable it becomes. When I go in on a "decomp" I bring all my equipment with me, camera, body bag, clipboard, stretcher. If I were to go back out into the fresh air and enter the death room again, my nose would have reset and I would once again be hit full-force by the smell.

I carry with me some odor blocker in small packets but have only used it once. The instructions indicate that a small amount should be smeared under the nose, but realistically, I think it needs to be shoved up both nostrils to be effective. The odor blocker gives off an aroma of baked bread, which is certainly preferable to Eau de Rotten Corpse.

So I guess the answer is…I just gag and deal with it.

When somebody dies on television or in the movies, it is usually preceded by a few poetic and well-chosen last words, followed by a deep sigh. Then the eyes close, the person stops breathing, and everybody cries. Most people who die suddenly don't have much time to compose an elaborate soliloquy, so their last words may be some variation of "Oh, shit" or "I can't breathe!" Yes, the eyes do seem to close at death about half the time, but what is usually not depicted on film is one of the more unpleasant but perfectly common aspects of death, losing control of your bladder and/or bowels. So the question is, "Am I going to crap my pants when I die?"

Maybe, but probably not. All sphincters release at death, including those controlling the bladder and the esophagus. As a funeral director friend of mine lamented one day, "You try to live your life with some dignity, and then they find you with a turd in your pants." Depending on the consistency of the stool (solid versus liquid) and the effect of gravity, bowel contents may be retained or expelled. Most bodies I have picked up have not emptied their bowels. However, many still pass gas upon moving, often loudly, longly, and stinkily.

However, even if you are lucky enough not to crap yourself at death, you will still most likely be a little damp down there. In most cases of sudden death, the bladder empties. This makes searching for a wallet or keys in a deceased person's pockets a bit unpleasant. When a person has been dying from a chronic illness over a period of weeks or days, the body may be so dehydrated as to no longer produce urine. I've noticed that victims of narcotic drug overdose often do not urinate at death. A pathologist explained to me that this is due to the drug's effect on the nerves that control the bladder.

Since the sphincter between the stomach and esophagus relaxes as well, the contents of the stomach often burble up, sort of a like a low-pressure vomiting. In the hours and days following death and the body begins to decompose, a dark, bloody substance called purge fluid exudes from the mouth as well. This is often erroneously thought to be due to trauma. In fact, it is a perfectly normal consequence of even natural death.

Purge fluid and loose bowels aside, there is really nothing quite as disgusting as a bloated, decomposed body. How does one go about moving a rotting corpse?

Very carefully. One of the first signs of early decomposition is a greenish discoloration of the lower right abdomen, in the area of the appendix, indicative of intestinal bacteria escaping and invading the rest of the body. At this stage, between one and three days after death, the outer layer of skin—the epidermis—will begin to separate from the lower layer—the dermis. Unfortunately, this is not always visible on the surface. I have grabbed an arm or a leg in an attempt to move a body and had the skin slough off in my hand. I would describe the sensation like rubbing your thumb on an over-ripe plum. This is highly unpleasant. It is best to use towels or sheets to grab limbs in these cases. As decomposition progresses, the skin completely separates and forms huge blisters, called skin blebs. Again, sheets are helpful, as are plastic sheets to wrap the body in. Yuck.

After I transport the seeping, purging, rotting, or bleeding remains back to the morgue or funeral home, what happens next? Does everybody get an autopsy? The answer is no. Only a select few do. In most cases of natural death, a person has had an illness for some time that would explain his or her death. The deceased person usually takes medications and has a physician who has seen that person regularly and is willing to sign the death certificate. In cases of a person who is found dead and has not seen a physician recently and/or has no significant medical history, an autopsy is usually performed. A pathologist or coroner would sign the death certificate in that case. In the cases of accidental and suicidal deaths, autopsies are usually performed, depending on local protocols. Homicides are always autopsied.

# Small-Town Funeral Parlor

I first met my next employer one evening on a cold night, down a long driveway, on Bainbridge Island, a bedroom community of Seattle in the Puget Sound. We had each been dispatched to the residence for different reasons, different missions. I was an EMT and my job was to try to make the dead guy come back to life. Dick's job was to take over after I had failed at my job.

Along with several other firefighters, I had helped move the man's body onto a gurney and conveyed him down the stairs to the aging Dodge minivan I would soon come to know as Old Smeller. Since I had some free time and a willingness to help, I offered my services to Dick as a removal technician. Several months later, he called me back and offered me some part-time work, probably because I knew how to use a gurney and had seen some dead people. This made me instantly more qualified than the next guy, I suspect.

So I bought a few cheap suits and shoes that were both practical and, I hoped, not a complete embarrassment to my vocation. Looking good was important, but so was not ruining your shoes slogging down a muddy driveway on a removal, or first call, as it was also known. A silk tie could be a nice touch, but not terribly practical when leaning over an oozing body, so I often omitted this detail, except at funeral services, where more formal dress was required.

Before long, I was not only removing and transporting the dead, I was also helping to dress and casket them. (Yes, casket is also a verb.) I even moved from behind the scenes to the forefront, becoming an apprentice funeral director, and helping to conduct many funerals and graveside services. Burials were usually pretty sedate, predictable affairs, with the exception of one I conducted in which the town drunk wandered by, howling, "I love you, Grandma!"—he wasn't related to the deceased—and then teetered on the edge of the grave. Disaster was averted by several relatives of the deceased, who yanked the drunk from the precipice, and escorted him a distance away, where he proceeded to sulk behind a tombstone for the remainder of the service.

The best part, perhaps, of my funerary career was driving the lumbering white hearse with the gleaming Landau bars on the back. It drove like a dream and parked like a Sherman tank. Piloting this beast through town was like being on stage in a morbid play—a stylish, if ghoulish reminder of the universality of mortality. My wife hated the thing; it spooked her. To this day, she averts her eyes when one passes by. At times her panic has been so severe, she has had to pull over to the side of the road and wait for her heart to beat regularly again.

# Mom, Lend a Hand

The van is in the shop, so we've got the hearse this evening. The nineteen-foot long Cadillac Victoria hums along Highway 305 toward the Little Boston Indian Reservation, where we are to make the removal of a man who was found dead in bed this afternoon. My fellow removal tech, James, rides beside me in his gray suit. The hearse, with its red velvety interior, smells much the same as my grandfather's Cutlass Supreme did, of leather and cleanliness. The aroma is distinctly different than that of our van, Old Smeller, a Plymouth Voyager with the ever-present but faint odor of death combined with overtones of alcohol hand sanitizer, embalming fluid, and long-forgotten flowers. It was a comfortable odor, in a weird way.

Prior to leaving the funeral home, we had taken a gurney out of the prep room and loaded it into the back, along with an ankle tag and a box of gloves. We did, however, lack a backboard or a body bag, items that are sometimes useful in tight spots. Using a hearse to do a home removal wasn't routine, but we had no other logical choice.

The only information we had, written down on a scrap of paper, was the address, the name of the dead man, and the approximate weight—four hundred pounds. I was hoping the police would offer to help us move the body, but, as I have learned, that is never a sure thing.

As we approach our destination, the scenery changes. Two-story houses with landscaped yards give way to moss-covered single-wide mobile homes and dilapidated and ancient travel trailers. We are now on the reservation. Pontiacs and Fords, old and ponderous, some of which haven't run since the turn of the century, line the weedy gravel driveways. Rusted lawnmowers, scrap metal, discarded and mildewed furniture, and broken flower pots sit, frozen in time, among the tall blades of grass that had taken over the majority of what once passed for a yard. It was the accoutrements of institutionalized poverty, the yards of people who never moved more than a mile away from the homes where they were born and seemed content to just exist.

The dark blue police SUV parked outside a multi-family dwelling, along with ten or so people milling about in the yard, indicates the dead man's residence. I position the hearse along the curb, grab my clipboard with the first call sheet clipped to it, and James and I walk towards the front door.

Tribal members have set up camp in the front yard, a weed-strewn patch of off-green in front of the one-story dwelling. Small children chase each other and a matronly woman of about sixty has brought food. Death is a spectator event here.

A stocky female police officer with lieutenant stripes below her shoulder patch leads us through the front door into a dimly lit man-cave of a living room, dominated by a massive flat-screen TV. The floor feels sticky below my feet and I notice multiple crushed Coors Light cans haphazardly strewn about, some on a rickety table, the others behind a worn and threadbare couch. I narrowly avoid hitting my head on a strip of flypaper that had already claimed multiple winged victims. The house smells dank and unventilated.

"What's the story?" I ask.

"This guy was drinking with his buddies till late at night, watching the game. Then he stumbled into the back room to sleep. He didn't wake up this morning when his friends came to check on him," she says.

"Have you found next of kin?"

"An aunt. I've got her phone number written down."

James and I make our way down a short, dark hallway and open the door that the lieutenant indicates. The door opens inwardly, but only halfway, as there is something in the way—the body. I turn sideways to squeeze through the narrow aperture into the room.

An immense middle-aged man lies on his back on a bare, stained mattress. A vomit-stained white T-shirt barely contains his abdominal girth and he is naked from the waist down, with the exception of socks. His legs are bent at the knees and his feet touch the floor. To his left, a pair of cast-off underwear lies in a heap, soiled with feces.

Why so many people choose to die in such inconvenient spots, I will never know. One removal technician I used to work with, a heavy man himself, said he would like to die in his attic after having stacked up furniture in front of the door, just to make things interesting for the funeral workers.

"The door will have to come off," I say. "Anybody have a screwdriver?"

The male police officer goes out to the crowd outside to see if anyone has any tools. A few minutes later, two younger Native men come in with tools to take the door off its hinges. While we wait, James and I move the gurney inside, lower it, and unzip the cot cover. We can only get it as far as the living room, since it wouldn't make it into the bedroom, even with the door off.

After the door is removed, it is time for the unpleasant and logistically difficult task of moving the body off the bed and onto the gurney. Since the man wears nothing but a T-shirt, there is nothing to grab hold of, and this necessitates the use of a tarp or blanket to go underneath him and slide him on the floor towards the gurney. A dead body isn't worth risking our backs. The standard plastic liners we usually use are not strong enough to hold four hundred pounds.

I walk outside and ask the throng for assistance. "Does anyone have a tarp we could use?"

A woman leaves and comes back a few minutes later with a new Pendleton wool Indian blanket. It seems a shame to waste it, as she will never want it back after it is used but the woman seems willing to donate to the cause.

By this time, the door is off its hinges and we are ready to move the body.

I rehearse the plan with the police officers and the two neighbors who have offered to help. "James and I will roll him towards us, then you shove the blanket underneath him, and then we will roll him back," I say.

As James and I strain to turn the flaccid bulk of the dead man, two rather disgusting, but not entirely unexpected events occur: First, the man burbles up dark fluid, known as purge, from his mouth, and then, as the female police officer tucks the blanket underneath his bottom, he issues a long, loud, extraordinarily smelly fart.

"Give me a minute," says the lieutenant, and quickly steps out of the room.

The male officer says, "I think we've lost her." We continue without her assistance, eventually getting the body onto the blanket and slid onto the floor. With five of us dragging, we move him into the living room and then heft him onto the gurney. We wrap him in the plastic liner, but it isn't big enough to contain him. The top strap is also too short to buckle him in.

After zipping up the cot cover, we wheel the body towards the hearse, our cargo jiggling precariously like Jell-O.

Once we are out in the open, all eyes are on us. It is as though we are on stage. This is never a good time to screw up and do something disastrous, like drop the body, or bang the dead man's head into a door. Families and friends have a tendency to remember those things.

42

Thankfully, all goes well, and James and I drive back to the funeral home, a little rumpled, red-faced, and sweaty.

Now comes the even more challenging part—sliding, pushing, shoving, yanking, or rolling four hundred pounds of dead flesh onto a narrow porcelain embalming table. What makes the task even more difficult is the prospect of placing plastic blocks underneath the torso and head so as to elevate the body and allow water, blood, and embalming fluid to flow freely around it and down the tiny drain at the bottom of the table.

I coat the edge of the embalming table with liquid soap in an attempt to make it more slippery. James grabs a leg, I grab an arm, and, with an indelicate thump, we heft our client onto the table.

"We need to get these blocks underneath him," I say.

James gives me a look that indicates this task is not high on his list of priorities. "I guess," he says.

I move to the man's left side and reach over to pull his right arm up, in an attempt to get him onto his side. James attempts to push the plastic block underneath but gets only as far as a shoulder before he is stopped by sheer mass. He shoves, but the dead, unyielding flesh prevents him from accomplishing his task. If it were any less morbid, this whole scenario might be funny—two small men in suits attempting to move a giant, completely uncooperative, dead man.

We stand back and breathe heavily before deciding it isn't worth the trouble. I turn on the fan that blows cold air into the room, slowing decomposition, before turning off the lights and shutting the door.

On my way home, I pass by the Bainbridge Library, where my parents are attending a lecture given by a man who wrote a book on being homeless. I'm feeling a bit guilty about leaving the body on the table without blocks, making it very difficult for Dick to complete the embalming in the morning.

43

"Dad, would you mind helping me with a body down at the funeral home?" I ask.

"I don't think so. I don't want to hurt my back again."

My mom, sixty-seven years old and all of one hundred and twenty pounds, pipes up, "I'll help!"

"Are you sure?" This is an unpleasant task for anyone, let alone someone whose contact with death has been minimal.

"Yes, I'm sure," Mom says with some hesitation in her voice.

We travel down to the funeral home. Once we are in the embalming room, Mom stands at the door, unsure of this task. "What do I do?" she asks.

"Here, put on this gown and these gloves."

I'm beginning to feel increasingly guilty about dragging my poor mother into this awful task. Mom struggles into her paper suit, looking particularly uncomfortable.

Mom wants to be cremated when her time comes, a fact that she has stated to me on numerous occasions. "I'll finally be warm!" she has said.

The idea of being pumped full of chemicals, painted up, and put on display fills Mom with revulsion. Despite my having explained to her that funerals are for the living, she has chosen to take her privacy and reserve with her to the grave, or to the niche, in this case. Her wish is to be cremated, her ashes placed in a niche at the rear of the church she has attended for going on forty years, and for there to be a quiet service to memorialize her. It was the wish of her parents as well, no-nonsense Episcopalians, not wanting to make a fuss either in life or in death.

Of the two options of burial or cremation, our large customer has chosen the former, or rather his tribe has chosen for him. His fellow tribal members, most of whom are also relatives, will gather together in an auditorium, dressed in casual clothing, and pass by his casket. They will place their hands on his still chest and kiss his cold forehead. And when the service ends, they will form a line behind his casket and escort him to his final resting place at the tribal cemetery. Shovelful by shovelful, his brothers and cousins and uncles will fill in the grave by hand.

As I turn the man to the side and Mom prepares to shove under the plastic blocks, the man's bowels let loose and a rivulet of diarrhea dribbles onto the porcelain. Mom gags. "This is really gross," she says.

Indeed it is, and Mom's efforts to slide the blocks under the fat folds prove about as effective as using a crayon to write on a balloon. A lift would be most helpful, but since we don't have one, we are left to give up, turn off the lights, and let the mountainous man lie there until morning when, with any luck, somebody with more strength or knowledge will come up with a solution to the problem.

Alas, when Dick opened the door the next morning and saw the task ahead of him, he almost immediately called a trade embalmer in do the work for him—a sort of rent-a-mortician, who offers his services to multiple mortuaries. I imagine the trade embalmer's work involved much sweat, towels, and swearing, but the job got done, as the man was eventually embalmed and laid in his casket for his viewing and burial. I thought he had looked a bit constipated, but it is darn difficult to get a four hundred-pound man wearing a suit to look decent lying on his back.

# Setting Features

Marilyn has been yawning since early this morning, when she died in a local nursing home. She yawned all through the removal, her mouth gaping open in an expression reminiscent of Edvard Munch's *The Scream*. She kept yawning as she was being wrapped in plastic, and, to my knowledge, all the way back to the funeral home. When I placed her on the embalming table, her expression didn't change. She looked bored with the whole process, her eyes half-open, irises directed slightly upwards as if to express her irritation with all the jostling.

I knew Marilyn was dead, but I didn't want her to look dead, and neither did the cadre of family members coming to bid her adieu at some time in the next several hours. The family wanted her to look as though she were asleep, the ultimate goal of any embalmer.

For several years, I held the distinction of intern embalmer/funeral director. The process to become an intern—the modern term for an apprentice—was simpler than obtaining a food handler's permit. The fact that I worked under the license of a fully qualified funeral director/embalmer enabled me to learn how to prepare a body for burial, handle arrangements, and assist with other aspects of disposition.

An essential element of embalming is the task known as setting features. When a person dies, all muscles relax. This causes the mouth to yaw open and the eyes to assume a half-closed position, generally not the effect desired by families who are to view the body. Setting features involves various techniques of closing and keeping closed the eyes and the mouth, providing the illusion of sleep. As there are several methods of doing this right, there are innumerable ways of doing it wrong. If the mouth is closed too tightly, the lips will curl into a scowl. Too loosely, and the expression will be one of boredom. The most popular method of mouth-closing involves the use of a needle injector, a device that shoots metal wires through the upper and lower jaw with a rather disturbing "ka-chunk" sound. The two wires are then twisted together. A second method involves threading a needle through the mouth and the nose and securing the mouth with twine. It was this method that my director preferred.

An embalming textbook had described the desirable setting of the eyes—closed, with the upper eyelid covering 2/3 of the globe and the bottom eyelid covering the lower 1/3. There are a few methods of closing eyes, including stuffing small wads of cotton beneath the eyelids or the use of commercially produced devices known as eye caps, convex pieces of plastic with tiny spikes designed to catch on the lids and keep the eyes from popping open.

Marilyn is proving difficult. Her age, ninety-four, has contributed to a general breakdown of the tissues, including those in her mouth. Again and again I thrust the needle through the fragile tissue and it keeps pulling through. The other challenge is her complete lack of teeth, which have caused an atrophy of the gums and jaw. I will need to use a mouth former, a plastic device resembling a hockey player's mouth guard, to compensate for her lack of teeth and fill out her sunken cheeks.

Finally, I'm able to get the tissue to hold, and I continue the suture by passing the needle between Marilyn's upper gums and lip and into the backside of her nose. The curved needle emerges out her left nostril. I then pass the needle through the septum, into the right nostril, and direct it back down into the mouth, completing the suture. After putting the mouth former in place, I gently close the jaw and knot the twine, stuffing the remainder into her mouth. Marilyn's lips close naturally over her newly formed expression, one of peace instead of horror.

Next, I open a jar of Kalon cream, a sort of postmortem beauty mask that will prevent the inherent dehydration in those folks whose cells no longer maintain homeostasis. Using a small paint brush, I slather the opaque cream over Marilyn's closed eyelids, nose, mouth, forehead, cheeks, and ears. With her head on a block, her eyes and mouth closed, and her hands folded over her abdomen, her features have been set, and she is ready for the next phase of embalming, arterial injection, performed later today by my much more experienced supervisor, Dick.

Setting features is primary in what those in the business refer to as creating a "memory picture." Since embalming hardens and dehydrates tissues, if feature setting is done improperly, it is impossible to fix it afterwards. Along with washing the body with germicidal soap, feature setting sets the stage for the injection of a variety of chemicals into the circulatory system to preserve, sanitize, and rejuvenate dead tissue.

I recall finishing a removal for another funeral home east of the mountains, Telford's Chapel of the Valley. We were to perform the embalming and then ship the body for casketing and viewing several days in the future. Unfortunately, there had been a windstorm, and power was out to the funeral home. Even more unfortunately, there existed no back-up generator and the preparation room was windowless, so I had to go to work by flashlight. Spraying off dried-on shit, alone, in the dark, is one of those existential moments that make a person question the trajectory of one's life work. I'm also lucky I didn't stab myself with the needle while suturing the mouth shut, mostly by feel.

Morticians are, in fact, master illusionists. Through the injection of chemicals into the arteries, inert tissue takes on an artificial vitality. Humectants combat the effects of dehydration. Rose-tinted dyes replace the sallow gray of death with the subtle pink of life. Specialized chemicals counteract the effects of jaundice, massive swelling, and chemotherapy. A cancer patient's sunken cheeks can be filled out once again by injecting gel under the skin, restoring an image of health, even youth, sort of a postmortem Botox treatment. I have even seen postmortem restorations appear to make a body seem ten years younger. So if you can't afford a facelift while still breathing, just wait a while, and it can be done when you are dead for a fraction of the cost.

A typical embalming might provide two weeks of good preservation, enough time for the family to gather and say their final goodbyes. If longer preservation is needed or if the body has decomposed some to begin with, chemicals used are more concentrated, allowing for a more extended period of viability. The downside to this is dehydration, and after a time, dark spots begin to appear on the face and hands as the tissue loses all its moisture. It becomes increasingly harder to mask this effect with cosmetics. However, some bodies, like those of civil rights leader Medgar Evers, have been exhumed after decades and are still viewable, though this is the exception to the rule. Mildew and a variety of colorful molds take over as the body lies underground, exposed to damp conditions. A condition called saponification, or adipocere formation, occurs in the presence of dampness. The fat of the body turns into a hard, soapy substance. This can sometimes be seen in bodies immersed in water for long periods of time.

Part of my job working for the Seattle-based mortuary service was to remove bodies from small funeral homes and transport them back to our facility for cremation. I once removed a rather malodorous body that had been marinating in a cooler for three months at a funeral home south of Seattle, but that experience didn't even begin to compare with that of my girlfriend at the time, who also was a removal technician. She had backed her van into the garage at our mortuary, stepped out, and asked somebody else to please remove the body from her van, lest she vomit. It seems that she had been sent to this same funeral home on a mission to rid them of a gentleman who had been slowly disintegrating on their prep table for the past year. The man was, in theory, embalmed, and still wearing the suit he was dressed in a year prior, but was beginning to liquefy. The family had never paid for his burial, and so there he lay in the prep room, a silent witness to all the goings-on in the funeral home for the past year, as everybody hustled and bustled around him, shifting caskets, embalming other bodies, and trying to ignore the fact that he was decomposing in their midst.

One of the apprentice embalmers, Craig, had opened the bag, looked at the poor fellow's rotting remains, and asked the question: "What did they embalm him with? Tap water?"

It was always a creepy experience to be in the prep room of that funeral home, located in the unmarked garage of an elderly house with flaking white paint. It had all the makings of a horror movie set: dim lighting, faint odor of decomposition, caskets haphazardly stacked on top of dressing tables and upended in the corner, and a large diagram of all the arteries and veins in the body displayed next to a rather old Porti-boy embalming machine. The only thing missing was the organ music. I could almost imagine Dr. Frankenstein at work in that dimly lit space, re-animating his monster.

In stark contrast to the rather undesirable conditions under which she worked, the undertaker of this particular establishment was a down-right friendly, animated woman who once greeted me with "Hi, honey!" as she rolled open the door to her dungeon. I'd never before met her.

When all preparations have been completed, and Mrs. McGillicuddy lies in her casket, her hair coiffed just so, her makeup impeccable, wearing her favorite dress from forty years ago, we may gaze upon her and say such things as, "Doesn't she look natural?" and, "She looks just like she's sleeping," never mind that most folks don't choose to sleep in a rectangular box wearing clothing ill-suited for sleeping. It seems that pajamas might be a better choice.

Embalmed bodies are weird creatures, the incorruptible saints of modern day, mere stand-ins for the persons they used to be, their skin cold, unyielding, and dehydrated. As the formaldehyde gas permeates every cell of the body, the tissue turns to gel. The stench of death is replaced with the odor of an anatomy lab, sterile and acrid. More mannequins than human remains, embalmed bodies are like elaborate full-body costumes, cleverly disguising death as mere stillness.

What lies beneath the thin veneer of cosmetics and neck to ankle clothing is anything but peaceful. Mrs. McGillicuddy's mouth has been sewn shut, her blood replaced with formaldehyde, and her internal organs poked full of holes by the wicked device known as a trocar. So much for Rest in Peace.

The illusion produced by morticians is one of sleep. With the exception of an occasional odd family who wishes to have their loved one displayed astride a motorcycle or seated at a kitchen table with a cigarette between two stiff fingers, bodies are displayed horizontally. In larger funeral homes, bodies "repose" in "slumber rooms." The analogy of sleep permeates not only the funeral industry's lexicon, but the lexicon of modern society. Rest in Peace. Grant to the departed eternal rest. The Big Snooze.

# Grandma's Last Trip

Today my grandmother died, and I removed her body. I've never before been so personally invested in a removal as I have today. We had known for some time that her time was short, and I had made a silent promise to Grandma that I would see her through to the very end.

At ninety-five years old, she was dying of what I could best describe as a general fatigue of life. She had been living in retirement homes for some time, had some dementia, but was able to function semi-independently. Her days consisted of sitting in her chair and reading large-print books, napping, and making frequent trips down the hallway to either the community library or to retrieve a Styrofoam cup full of luke-warm, low-grade coffee from a machine that had been turned off hours prior. She had seemed content, though not necessarily happy.

She had eaten "like a bird" as my mother put it, for many months, and it had seemed inconceivable to me that a human body could continue to exist for so long on so few calories. What she did eat was mostly candy, of which I made sure she had plenty every Christmas in a basket stuffed full of crackers, cheese, and chocolates. Still, she plodded along, enjoying more Christmases than we could have anticipated, surviving cancer twice, and burying two husbands along the way. My dad's father had died when I was still a baby and when Grandma married again years later, she married a man much younger, vowing that she would never again be a widow. Ed died anyway, leaving Grandma in search of a new place to live. For a while, she lived with my parents at their home, and then, as her health progressively worsened, she went to an assisted living facility, and then another, and then another. Dad said he thought she might be immortal, and I was beginning to believe it also.

One day, Grandma did nothing but sat and stared at her dinner, then walked back to bed, and never got up again. Within a few days, she was put on hospice care and I visited more frequently, as did my father and my wife, who had taken on my family as her own. On several occasions my wife would rise early and drive the half-hour from our town to Silverdale and sit at Grandma's bedside, watching her sleep, holding her hand.

On the morning she passed from this earth, I was on my way to work. My wife was at her bedside when it happened. She called me as I was on the ferry boat to the mainland.

"I'm sitting with Grandma. Her eyes are dark. I think this is her last day."

"Should I turn around and come home?"

"You probably should. I don't think she'll be here much longer." She paused and then said, "She just took a deep breath."

"I'm turning around and getting back on this ferry as soon as we hit Edmonds."

"I think she's gone, Matt. I can't feel a pulse. I've never seen anyone die before."

I call my work and give them the news. Then I drive off the ferry and get right back into line to go back to Kingston. I couldn't be with my grandmother as she died, but I could be there to support my family.

When I arrive at the home, my wife and father are keeping vigil over grandma's body. Eyes sunken and skin stretched over facial bones, she doesn't look at all like herself. Her skin is tinged a sickly yellow. This is death, natural, normal at the end of ninety-five years, the same look of death I had seen hundreds of times before. But now it's personal. This is somebody I love.

Wordlessly, I pull the bouquet of flowers from the vase beside her and lay several long-stemmed roses on Grandma's still chest. I place her cold hands atop the flowers and hug her for a minute, tears flowing down my cheeks.

When Ibrahim from the funeral home arrives, he stands in the doorway for a few moments and looks as though he is about to cry.

Ibrahim and I work silently, attaching a name band to Grandma's ankle and then turning her so as to place a plastic sheet underneath her. Her back is purple with lividity, the postmortem settling of blood due to gravity. Crinkling plastic is the only sound as we place her on the cot. She is covered now from head to toe, *really dead*.

Rain comes down in sheets as Ibrahim and I wheel the cot to the waiting van—a perfectly gloomy atmosphere for the circumstances, gray sky, wet pavement, and silence.

We drive another hour to the crematory in Kent, a drab, industrial building that bears no outward signs of the business run within. Ibrahim backs the van into the dim garage where the crematory machines hum away and the acrid odor of cremated remains hangs in the air. Dark-suited technicians stand ready to take Grandma into their care.

I wheel our cot alongside a mechanical lift with a sheet of plywood on top. An imposing black man in an all-black suit stands by to whisk her from one to the other. With a soft thump, he slides her to the plywood.

"This is my grandmother," I say unnecessarily. Why I feel this is pertinent, I do not know. Did I expect the tech to treat grandma with more care as a result of this knowledge? Or was I simply asking for him to acknowledge my great loss.

"Yes, I know," he says simply, and goes to work taping the plastic together into a bundle using a tape dispenser. As the last gray hair disappears into the plastic wrap, I am acutely aware that I will never see her again. She has now become a package, like to many others destined very soon to be placed on a shelf in the massive refrigerator, and later, packed in cardboard, then slid into a blazing hot crematory retort. She will be returned to us a week or two later, not in grandmother form, but as eight pounds of ground bone and ash encased in a non-descript rectangular plastic container.

Having outlived most of her family and two husbands along the way, there are few to mourn and no funeral to plan. Her remains are spread in a park in Oregon, where her first husband's, my grandfather's, ashes were spread years before. A priest attends, and my parents, but they are the only ones.

As Ibrahim drives back home, another removal already on his schedule, I gaze out the windshield and watch the rain splatter the freeway. The one we called Immortal was now dead, as were so many others whose bodies I had removed in the past. My sweet wife Kenzie was there for her final moments, and I had fulfilled my silent promise to her that I would see her to the very end.

# Burial or Cremation?

Paper or plastic? Smoking or non-smoking? Decaf or regular? The question to me is a matter of preference, devoid of moral or ethical value judgment. What does my family want? Are we a traditional family or a cremation family?

Traditional burial is not "green" in the least. Each year, thousands of gallons of embalming fluid and tons upon tons of steel, wood, and concrete, are placed in the ground for eternity. The practice of traditional burial is still the most popular in this country, with the stronghold still remaining in the south, where in many places the idea of forgoing a wake and "Christian burial" is anathema. In the states of Washington and Arizona, for example, cremation leads the way, with 70% of all dead people going up in smoke.

I come from the Episcopal tradition, and Episcopalians cremate. No fanfare, all practicality. My parents have already picked out their double-occupancy niche in the columbarium behind St. Barnabas Episcopal Church on Bainbridge Island. My maternal grandparents' ashes reside in a church wall. The remains of my paternal grandparents have been spread to the four winds. The mortal remains—or cremains, as they are also known—of our beloved pet cat, Custard, have been sitting on a shelf in my parents' house for years now. They will be interred with the first of my parents to die. To my knowledge, my brother will end up there as well.

My wife comes from a "traditional family," Catholics that have buried their dead for generations, but there is no guarantee she will outlive me. My daughter, now a small child, may likely choose the post-mortem fate of both of her parents. I wouldn't deign to guess her choice, but ultimately, it will be up to her and those others left behind. I won't care. My spirit will be light years away.

Cremation has become more popular, in part, because it is much less expensive than traditional burial, the idea that it is considered eco-logically more "friendly," and the fact that families are now spread far apart across the nation. An eight-pound box of ground bone and ash can be distributed amongst several "keepsake urns" and kept on shelves, worn around the neck on a pendant, or even made into a diamond.

With cremation, one can be blown into outer space, scattered in one's favorite park, buried, interred, committed to a water burial in an "earth urn," or simply forgotten on a shelf.

I once had the unusual occasion of serving a client who had chosen both cremation and burial for himself. In the hospital, he had had both legs amputated. Wanting to be buried whole, he requested that his legs be cremated and then, later, when the rest of him had died, the ashes would be placed in his casket. I had wheeled my cot into the morgue and then placed the plastic-covered limbs into the pouch and zipped it up, just as I would a complete body. The only question was how to label the bag—"Mr. Smith's Legs?" Would each leg get a toe tag?

Few images are as indelible as the first time one witnesses a flaming skull. In the process of cremation, the remains need to be "stoked" pe-riodically, and this necessitates the opening of the heavy steel door to the retort, revealing a burning skeleton, the skull, pelvis, and long bones still readily recognizable, but glowing bright orange.

The first time I set foot inside a crematory, I was immediately struck by the unmistakable odor of combusted flesh. It wasn't an un-pleasant odor, though it was distinctive, and I have recognized it imme-diately in many funeral homes and crematories since. The crematory resembled a warehouse, the floors, ceiling, walls, and equipment covered by a thin coating of black soot. The twin cremation machines rumbled, massive people-eating furnaces. Beside both lay cremation trays, bearing the products of cremation—still recognizable bones. Occasionally, a titanium hip replacement. Against the wall is a fifty-gallon garbage can, overflowing with artificial joints, titanium plates, screws, and various other hardware. When the can is completely stuffed, it will be sent to a local recycling center.

Occasionally, something goes wrong. I recall one day when the crematory owner, Jerry, placed a body into the retort and closed the door. There was an almost immediate "whump!" sound, accompanied by a puff of black smoke escaping from all corners of the door.

"See, it's not supposed to do that," said Jerry, stating the obvious. Later in the day, we received a surprise visit from the fire department, investigating a smoke complaint. Apparently, a plume of smoke had erupted from the chimney and descended over the neighborhood.

In contrast to the industrial feel of a crematory, an embalming room, where the preparation for burial takes place, has the feeling of a surgical suite. The air is cool and smells of a mixture of formalin-based fluid and the massage cream used to soften and hydrate the skin of those bound for viewing.

A typical funeral and burial can cost upward of $15,000 and is a relative rarity in Washington State, where I live and work. Cremation hovers at about 70%. A few choose to donate their bodies to science, and a few are shipped off to other states for burial. It seems that Catholics and Mormons keep the traditional funeral alive, so to speak, as they are they are the only ones that consistently bury their dead. The Catholic Church has relaxed its stance on burial in recent years, but the priest almost always prefers the body to be present in the church during the service, whether the casket is open or remains closed throughout.

From the perspective of the funeral director, the preparation for a funeral is extensive. The body must be embalmed, dressed, and cosmetized. If the deceased is a woman, a hairdresser may need to be called in. If the deceased is a victim of trauma that affects the face, "restorative art" may need to be performed, involving wax, possibly injections of "tissue builder" under the skin, and even plaster to rebuild a shattered skull.

Newspapers must be contacted for obituaries. The cemetery must be contacted as well as the vault company for opening and closing of the grave. Prayer cards and service leaflets must be ordered from the printer. A casket must be ordered. The hearse and any service car used must be washed. The death certificate must be completed and then filed.

At the funeral itself, the director acts as a master of ceremonies, wrangling pallbearers, ushering mourners into the church and leading them out, opening and closing the casket, and coordinating with clergy, notorious for having their own ideas as to how to run a funeral. The organist and clergy must be paid, flowers must be ferried to the church and then to the graveside, and everything must be done with utmost of decorum and efficiency.

When the casket is placed in the grave, the dirt is shoveled over the casket, and the turf replaced, the dead may rest forever, often in much the same condition as when they were buried. With good embalming, proper soil conditions, and a quality casket, bodies may be fully recognizable, even viewable after being underground for twenty years.

A friend and co-worker of mine, long dead of a heart attack, rests six feet underground in a cemetery in Portland, Oregon. Sometimes I imagine him, still dressed in his dark suit, with his hair still perfectly coiffed, lying perfectly still in his casket, frozen in time, through season after season, year after year.

# Investigations

After several years of working part-time for two different funeral homes, I got the opportunity to combine my medical knowledge with my mortuary experience and become a deputy coroner in 2009. As with most events in my life, I arrived at this job serendipitously, if a bit tragically.

One of my fellow paramedics, who also served as a deputy coroner, had the misfortune to suffer a massive heart attack and die one evening, leaving a vacancy for his part-time position at the coroner's office. I decided that it might be poor form to approach the coroner at this fellow's funeral, so I waited a couple of months before coming in for the most informal interview I ever remember.

"Just get me a copy of your resume," the coroner had said. "In case HR wants it at some point."

This I did, and then we sat down, briefly discussed my experience or lack thereof, and the coroner handed me the keys to the van and plugged me into the schedule. Well, it wasn't quite that simple, but it seemed that way at the time. At present, the selection process involves a multi-page application, resume, criminal background check, rating process, and a formal interview, with possibly feats of strength to be added at some time in the future.

I rode along with the coroner on fewer than five calls, attempted to learn the ins and outs of the computers, fax machine, morgue protocol, toxicology, and the intricacies of the digital camera. The camera caused me the most consternation, as I would frequently take it out on a call, find it was in some weird mode I didn't recognize, fumble around while the police officers watched me, plead for help, and then snap a few blurry photos to the vexation of my supervisor.

But eventually I had enough knowledge to be almost dangerous, though the learning curve remained steep for several months thereafter. I've made a few missteps along the way, but I've also discovered a passion for finding the truth, whether it comes from a good field investigation, or from a full autopsy.

As a death investigator for Skagit County, on the damp side of Washington, two hours north of Seattle, I spend much of my on-duty time at home, my camera case and jacket by the door, waiting for my phone to ring with 911 dispatch reporting a death. Since we aren't a very busy office, I have the opportunity to respond to most field deaths that a larger office wouldn't have the time or resources to respond to—apparent natural deaths, folks with significant medical history. Even if there wasn't a suspicion of foul play, it was still rewarding for me to be able to answer questions from a family about how their loved one died. I was writing the final chapter of their lives, which was an honor.

While most death scenes were fairly mundane and predictable, the double-edged sword of the job is that one minute I might be snoozing on the couch or walking the dog, the next I may be driving an hour into the wilderness to investigate an accident, a drowning, or even a homicide far off the beaten path.

# Frozen

My pager breaks the silence of a cold January day with its plaintive chirping. Through bleary eyes, I stare at the blue screen. "0800 hours: from: Detective Jones—Call me about a homicide."

I dial the number for Detective Jones and the first words out of her mouth are, "Got your snowshoes?"

*This doesn't sound good.*

"So," she continues, "we've got a woman shot to death. We're investigating it as a homicide. The scene is about a two-hour hike in after you get into Marblemount. It's below freezing and snowing, so dress warm."

"Hmmm," I say, unable to come up with a more intelligent remark at this hour.

"You can go up there with us, or you could just stay at the trailhead and we'll bring the body down to you."

As my neurons begin to make tentative connections with each other in my non-caffeinated state, I briefly consider the relative merits of each scenario: wait in my heated van for the homicide victim to be delivered to me like a UPS package or join in the great adventure of cross-country cold weather body retrieval. For reasons still baffling to me, I choose the latter.

I rise from bed, leaving my wife peacefully unaware of my departure. Forlornly, I stare at my still warm sheets and my sleeping wife and feel jealous, wondering when I am next going to see either the sheets or the wife. Then, shivering, I slip on the blue cargo pants and beige polo shirt of the Coroner's Office. I grab my clipboard, pager, and phone, and head out to my frost-covered van. Naturally, I forget completely about the whole "dress warmly" thing.

The van's windows are iced over so I give it a few minutes to warm up while I take my tiny dog out to do his tiny business. The day is clear but frigid, with a brisk breeze swaying the trees around the travel trailer I call home.

I make a pit-stop at a coffee stand and bathe my brain cells in caffeine. I'm addicted to the stuff, and if I go past noon or so without at least one cup, my head will feel as if it may explode.

As I head east on the rural highway, the sun is just beginning to rise above the high hills. I pass acres of pasture and Holsteins grazing, steam rising from their nostrils, carloads of weekenders getting an early start, kayaks mounted atop their SUVs, Starbucks in their hands, all oblivious to the mission of the unmarked forest-green county van driven by the groggy, bed-headed man clutching a coffee cup.

I'm going "Upriver," following the path of the Skagit River as it snakes through the small communities and vast verdant flanks of fir trees to the next county and the end of my jurisdiction. Folks go "Upriver" to disappear. From all over the nation, in obscure ways, the wanderers, the disenfranchised, and the pioneers find the socked-in hills and valleys of Concrete, Rockport, Birdsview, and Marblemount. It seems on nearly every case I respond to Upriver, I have trouble finding next of kin. Either there really aren't any, or the decedent has pissed off everybody close to them, making it nearly impossible to find anything that would lead me to family. I find myself scouring cabinets, dusty tables, and wallets for tiny scraps of paper with anything—phone numbers long disconnected, addresses, old Christmas cards—that might lead me to someone who might be willing to step up and take responsibility for final disposition.

Tarheels seemed attracted to the Upriver area, and at some point there seemed to have been a mass migration of North Carolinians to the area. Many Upriver folks might be described as hillbillies, self-sufficient, often unsophisticated, and, I have come to find, not huge fans of the medical establishment. A personal physician was usually called upon to sign a death certificate, though frequently there wasn't one, since, in the words of more than one Upriver denizen, "Damn doctors'll just make ya sicker."

It takes about an hour and a half just to get to the end of the county road where I am to meet with first responders. By now I am at least at a therapeutic level of caffeine.

Marblemount Fire Department's aging aid car idles in the cold morning air, sending exhaust clouds skyward. A weary volunteer mans the wheel, ready to take me to the trailhead to meet with deputies. I grab my camera, response bag, and jacket, and jump into the back.

Sheriff vehicles and a Skagit Mountain Rescue Unit await me when I arrive at the trailhead. In a brilliant stroke of absent-mindedness, I have forgotten my boots. Now the only footwear that I have is my simple slip-on duty boots.

A man dressed from head to toe in wool directs his gaze at my ill-advised footwear, and then up to the armful of equipment I'm carrying. "Is that how you're going up there?" he asks.

"Forgot my boots," I say.

"You do realize how far it is up there, don't you?" he says, his weathered face impassive. He drops his pack off his shoulder and onto the snow. "Here. Stow your camera in here and don't bother carrying that box. Do you have wool socks?"

"Uh, no," I say. I had simply left the trailer wearing my normal coroner response attire, ill-suited to the conditions. This is how people die, I remind myself, attempting to tackle the elements without the proper equipment or clothing.

Sheriff's Detectives Jones and Gunderson wear wool caps, heavy boots, and multiple layers. They are clearly prepared for the elements. Skagit Mountain Rescue appears to be ready for an avalanche, with their heavy packs and ski poles. I feel vastly under-prepared. Despite the obvious dangers of hypothermia or frostbite, foolish pride takes over and I take my place in the middle of the pack. Ahead of me, Skagit County Detectives and Mountain Rescue, behind me, two more members of Mountain Rescue, one with a heavy Stokes basket strapped to his back.

Fresh snow crunches beneath my boots as a light snow falls. The trail is only moderately steep, though snow-laden branches brush us constantly as we make our way up the narrow trail.

Just as it seems that our journey will be fairly easy, the Mountain Rescue Team member at the front shouts back to the rest of us, "We've got at least two streams to cross. We'll need to use our poles."

Within a half an hour, we come across the first stream. Icy glacier water rushes over glistening stones and an insubstantial-appearing narrow fallen log spans the distance. Apparently, this is what we will be using to cross. Mountain Rescue makes it to the other side first, followed by the rest of us, teetering across on the slippery log. One misstep could spell serious injury or death.

By some miracle, we all arrive on the other side unscathed. I am thankful my flimsy boots don't fill up with water. We tromp on.

After a time, it seems easy to forget the ghoulish mission we are all on, investigating and recovering the body of a homicide victim. We are simply acquaintances, out for a cross-country snowshoeing adventure, reveling in the bitter cold and light snowfall, looking forward to a blazing campfire and libations at journey's end.

As minutes turn into an hour and more, I am becoming aware that both feet have turned into blocks of ice, but I try to tell myself that it is of no consequence. I have been colder than this before, and I pay my numb digits no further mind.

An hour and a half into our journey, we get our first sign that we our nearing our destination—several other members of Mountain Rescue who have made it up the mountain before us, and are awaiting our arrival. They have been there since the early hours of the morning, are completely enveloped in cold-weather gear, and have been waiting so long that they have used to a camp stove to boil water and warm their feet. Icicles cling to their beards and "snot stalactites" encrust their mustaches.

We are led a few hundred yards more to the scene. In the midst of a shallow, snow-covered depression in the landscape sits a small tent, covered by a tarp secured at the corners by bungee cords and stakes. This is the death scene.

Detective Jones says, "Give us a few minutes to process the scene, and then you can come in and examine the body." It is protocol for law enforcement to conduct an investigation of the total scene, including taking measurements and finding bullet casings, before medical examiners are allowed to view the body. However, statutes prohibit anybody but the coroner or his representative from moving a body, except as needed for life-saving efforts or identification.

After shifting from foot to foot and milling about aimlessly in an effort to maintain body heat, detective Gunderson beckons me in.

As with any scene, I photograph the surroundings before moving on to the body. If I were to focus first on the body, it would be easy for me to disregard the totality of the scene and its contribution to how the decedent came to be in the position she was in.

An ax lies in the snow next to a nearly-empty bottle of Wild Turkey Whiskey. Apparently imbibing by fireside was on the menu for last night. Charred firewood is strewn nearby, along with a blood-smeared sleeping bag that appears haphazardly tossed aside. Various pieces of clothing are strewn about. The snow is heavily trodden. I am having more difficulty feeling my feet.

I lean inside the two-man tent where a young woman lies enveloped in a down sleeping bag, still, pale, and rapidly assuming atmospheric temperature, a semi-automatic handgun a few inches from her head on the floor, barrel pointed towards the body. A dark article of clothing is wrapped around her forehead and it appears to be soaked with blood. I reach out with gloved hands in an attempt to remove it but it is immobile and crusty in my grasp—frozen to her head. Long lashes accentuate her eyes, closed in death, purple-lidded, swollen shut. The wound is in her forehead. Her facial bones are destroyed, but I cannot see the wound, for the makeshift bandage on her head. I will leave it in place for the pathologist.

Later, we are to find out the rest of the story. Apparently, the young woman and her boyfriend had been drinking and target shooting. The victim had gone to bed and her boyfriend, three sheets to the wind, had settled in for the night later. He had retrieved his weapon from at the foot of his sleeping bag in order to store in under his pillow. Somehow, according to the boyfriend, he had managed to hit the trigger with his frozen, whiskey-addled hands, and shoot his girlfriend smack dab in the middle of the forehead. The odds of something like this happening were darn near impossible but…that was his story.

I unzip her sleeping bag to reveal a woman ready for the elements— multiple layers of thermal clothing, right down to her socks. As I check for the telltale signs of lividity on her back, I detect the slightest hint of body warmth still retained in these frigid conditions. I snap photographs of her face, her hands, her chest, and back. I look for additional wounds, signs of a struggle, and find none.

I back out of the tent and speak to Detective Jones. "Let's keep her in her sleeping bag and package her up like that." I am still unsure as to how we're going to get her down off the mountain over such rough terrain.

The detectives remove the gun and place it into an evidence bag. I place an identification tag on the dead woman's pale ankle, and ready her for transport. She is first wrapped in a homicide linen, a clean white sheet designed to retain biologic evidence that would otherwise be lost or degraded. I then zip her into a disaster pouch, the quintessential "body bag" depicted so often in films, black, formless, heavy, and morbid, with a zipper running down the side. Then Mountain Rescue disassembles the campsite, taking the tent and its contents into evidence. I place the dead woman as well as her backpack into a Stokes Litter, a wire mesh basket designed for rescue and recovery operations. Mountain Rescue then works on the task of securing her to the basket with heavy-duty ropes.

By now, Mountain Rescue has decided to evacuate the body via helicopter. They have called for Snohomish County Sheriff's Office to fly into the remote canyon and do a "short haul" to the nearest airport in the small, nearby town of Concrete. Detective Gunderson instructs emergency dispatch to send another coroner vehicle to the airport to rendezvous with the helicopter.

An older member of Mountain Rescue eyes me suspiciously. "Can you feel your feet?" he asks.

"Kind of."

"No. That's not good." He shakes his head vigorously. "Take off your boots."

Feeling as sheepish as a small boy who has had an accident in his pants, I remove my boots and socks. The older man kneels down and checks my toes for feeling and circulation: "Can you feel this?" He pinches my toe.

"Yes, I can feel you're pinching my toe."

"Here." He reaches into his backpack and produces a pair of gray

68

wool socks. "Put these on."

I do as I am told. Some rudimentary feeling begins to return to the ice blocks that had formerly been my feet. I'm glad that somebody is watching out for the totally unprepared Deputy Coroner.

With the body secured to the Stokes Litter and feeling barely beginning to return to my distal appendages, it is a matter of waiting for the helicopter to arrive.

Forty minutes or so later, the almost imperceptible whine of a helicopter can be heard in the crisp air. Tentatively and carefully, the pilot guides the ship through the tree-lined hills and into our view. Soon it is overhead, whipping up dry snow and creating a localized blizzard. A crew member descends with a line, and it is quickly secured to the litter. In moments, the body is aloft, swinging slightly as the chopper makes its way out of the ravine and towards the airport.

I still have the socks.

# Of Maggots and Men

Among the candidates for "my favorite insect," flies and their horrible little children, maggots, rank rather low on my list. At once both fascinating and revolting, maggots have been nature's little morticians for eons, munching happily on dead flesh and then loping away to pupate and become adult flies. Within hours of a death, the ubiquitous fly homes in on the smell of a dead body, like a shark to blood. A body left outside for even three hours may have what appears to be Parmesan Cheese in the nostrils and corners of the mouth—fly egg clusters, soon to become wiggling white maggots.

At first feeding on fluids exuding from mucous membranes and open wounds, the maggots go through three molts, or instars, before leaving the body to form a pupa. Through these molts, they increase in size and ferocity, ultimately burrowing underneath the skin to augment the natural process of decomposition. On a completely maggot-infested body, one can actually *hear the maggots eat*—the soft smacking sound of thousands of organisms wriggling over each other and chewing with their hook-like mouth parts while they continue to breathe through spiracles on their hind end. A body in advanced decomposition that has been exposed to fly activity will exhibit large balls of maggots, known as maggot masses, in the nose and mouth. These masses will actually generate their own heat.

As the time for pupation approaches, the mature maggots crawl off to form their cocoons. In nature, maggots find shelter under rotting leaves or other tree debris. In an urban apartment, they crawl to the baseboards and, if feasible, underneath rugs or clothing. When they emerge from the pupae, they are adult flies, and the life cycle starts again.

Needless to say, flies are unwelcome in a morgue or funeral home. As I was assisting with an open-casket funeral at a church, a well-meaning funeral attendant decided to open chapel doors on either side of the sanctuary, allowing "fresh air" to enter the church. The doors were quickly closed by the funeral director/embalmer who had prepared the body, as leaving them open would be like hanging a "Welcome" sign for the local fly population. A loved one gazing down at poor dear departed Grandma as a fly emerges from her left nostril generally does not make for a good "memory picture."

Maggots, the tricky little bastards, seem to be very good at infiltrating their local surroundings. Several months back, my pathology crew and I were completing an autopsy on a man found dead in a ravine. His remains consisted of a skeleton, a few lumps that resembled internal organs, and a thriving community of maggots swarming so fervently as to make the corpse appear alive. My task here apparently involved taking photographs as well as corralling the maggots as best as possible into a dustbin. Snap snap. Sweep sweep. Rinse. Lather. Repeat.

Upon completing the autopsy, limited though it was due to the degree of our client's degradation, we double-bagged the remains, and closed the cooler door with confidence, knowing that soon some poor funeral home employee would arrive to take possession of our malodorous customer.

Several days later, we received some complaints from office staff several yards down the hallway. It seemed that a few adventuresome maggots had gone on a field trip. This meant they would have needed to escape my broom and dustpan, enter the anteroom, slip under the door, and lope down the hallway undetected, until making their presence known to the Human Resources Department, probably to inquire about a job.

Lest I malign our wiggly friends too much, maggots are not entirely

71

useless creatures. When they aren't infesting my morgue, maggots are excellent recyclers of dead animals the world over. Furthermore, they have medical use. In the case of non-healing leg ulcers, medical-grade maggots (one wonders what qualifications a maggot would need for this honor) have been applied to the affected areas, and in a short time, are found to have gobbled up all of the dead flesh, leaving the living parts alone.

From a forensic standpoint, maggots have found use in the determination of the cause of death as well. Maggots feeding on a corpse may ingest the drugs that have been involved in a death. By putting a chunk of maggots into a blender and making a "maggot milkshake," these drugs may be isolated and tested. I've never done this particular technique, and I'm not in a hurry to rush out and buy a blender for the express purpose of pureeing maggots, but I include this only as an academic curiosity.

As the body degrades further, eventually the maggots run out of viable flesh and the flies stop laying eggs. The skin shrinks and dries, stretched over the bones like a leathery canvas, inviting other creatures, such as beetles, to feast on what is left.

Aside from the insect decomposers, ants, rats, and even family pets can inflict damage on a corpse, each with its own distinctive pattern of injury. Ants tend to produce an abrasion-like pattern with their tiny jaws, whereas rats create a neat, bloodless, scalloping wound, eventually producing an appearance reminiscent of an anatomical dissection. Dogs and cats, left hungry by their dead owners, can wreak havoc on a body, at times dismembering it and leaving parts throughout the house.

Sometimes, however, a death can be so lonely that even the flies aren't invited.

# The Man That Nobody Missed

The pager chirps to life, with impeccable timing, right as I breeze through the doors of Safeway, only caffeine in my stomach and hungry for solid food. The sky is gray and the asphalt is dry on a cold late January day. The acrid, yet intoxicating odor of freshly brewed coffee wafts from the Starbucks kiosk.

I press the button and read the message on the blue screen: "Contact Officer Williams. We have a death." I dial the number on the screen. A female voice answers: "We're at the President Hotel at an unattended death. Looks like he's been down...a while."

"How long is a while?"

"A week at least. Maybe more."

"I'll be there in about fifteen minutes."

I start the van and gird myself for the sight, and most especially the smell, of a decomposed human being, that nostril-searing funk that warns all within nose-shot to stay away, or risk losing your cookies. I go through my mental checklist of those items I need, starting with a heavy-duty, fluid-impermeable body bag and ending with the odor-blocking gel given to me by a now-deceased Deputy Coroner. The gel was supposed to be smeared under one's nose, and exude an aroma not unlike a bakery, allowing one, at least temporarily, to forget that one was in the presence of a rotting corpse, and instead imagine buttered croissants. I had yet to use the gel on an actual case.

I start the van and head right out of the parking lot, onto bustling

College Way and cars full of post-Christmas shoppers, past Denny's and Petco, under the freeway full of whizzing cars, and towards the old downtown area, where my "client" lies waiting for me.

I pull up to the curb beside the President Hotel, a run-down building long past its prime. After retrieving the yellow plastic case that contains my digital camera, I place it on the extra-wide heavy-duty gurney, and head into the building. The lobby smells of loneliness and age and is completely deserted. I board the elevator with my gear and head up to the second floor.

The smell hits me as soon as the elevator door opens to the second floor. It is clear something is definitely not right here. Faint at first, then increasing exponentially as I round the corner, the smell of death is unlike any other, thick, cloying, and immediately recognizable, the chemicals putrescine and cadaverine combining to create the ultimate miasma of foulness.

A detective, young, tall, and balding, stands outside the beat-up door to the apartment. Police standing outside a residence is often a very bad sign.

I introduce myself and walk into the modest, cluttered apartment, camera dangling around my neck. A small rickety table stands in the entryway, bearing a set of keys and a dented bowl containing spare change. The door frame is damaged, splintered from being kicked in. A large black fly buzzes aimlessly over kitchen counters dotted with food debris and littered with empty cans of cheap beer. The dirty white cabinet doors have been flung open to reveal several randomly arranged medication bottles. I pick one up, the label faded, the cap dirty and slightly tacky—Atenolol, a high blood pressure medication. Another is labeled Simvastatin, a cholesterol-lowering drug. A bottle labeled Vicodin 5/500 mg looks slightly newer. I make a rough estimate of the amount of pills left to make sure it is consistent with normal use and that the man had not overdosed. On the label is written a physician's

74

name and prescription date. Things are looking up. If the man has a verifiable medical history and has recently seen a physician, my job becomes easier. It becomes more likely that he has died of natural causes and his doctor would sign off on his cause of death. I take photographs of these and then toss them into a paper bag for disposal.

On the refrigerator, tacked on with a magnet, is a reminder notice from a physician's office, reading "Mr. Scott Warner is scheduled for an appointment January 11 at 10:00 a.m." The date is circled. I look at my cell phone and check the date: January 24. This man has likely been dead for at least thirteen days.

I photograph this and then ask the detective the pertinent questions: "When was Scott last seen alive and by whom?"

The detective says it's been about a month since anyone has spoken to the decedent. Finally a friend had knocked on his door, received no answer and called police for a welfare check. Next of kin? Still not known. An officer hands me a dilapidated address book that smells of cigarette smoke, its pages stained and dog-eared, along with a cell phone. These two items will be vital in finding the dead man's relatives.

With the living area, such as it is, photographed, it is time to move on to the body itself, the heart of the investigation. Sidestepping multiple unlabeled boxes in the narrow hallway, I make my way into the bedroom. The odor of death increases. The room is sparely furnished, a bare mattress squarely in the middle of the space, beside it a plastic bin that passes for a bedside table. Atop the bin is a tiny lamp, still on, its shade askew, illuminating an opened burger wrapper, flecked with cheese and ketchup, dried up. An ancient radio, now off, sits above an old steam radiator below an open window. It is the apartment of a transient, one who had recently moved in and had no plans of staying permanently.

Mr. Warner, or the remains thereof, reclines diagonally on the mattress, partially covered by a down sleeping bag, his sockless feet hanging off the side of the bed. His formerly Caucasian skin is black, which is not to say Negroid, but rather obsidian with the effects of decomposition, contrasted by the white whiskers that adorn his upper lip and cheeks to form a Fu Manchu mustache. A gray T-shirt is stretched over his ample upper body, made even larger by bloat. His eyes are squeezed shut, his fingers and toes dried and shriveled, mummified. Pajama bottoms, soaked with decomposition fluid, cover his lower body. As foul as he is, I need to examine him for signs of injury or foul play. My thickly gloved hands touch cold skin, sloughing off in my hand as I pull up his T-shirt and examine his chest and abdomen. No stab wounds, no bullet holes, just fluid-filled blisters, or bullae, of moderate to advanced decomposition.

The scene investigation completed, the property inventoried, and the medications accounted for, it is now time for the most odious task of all, the removal of Mr. Warner's decomposed body from his apartment. This will require the assistance of my less-than-enthusiastic law enforcement comrades.

"Ready to move him?" I say.

The officer suddenly remembers an old back injury, and the two detectives grumble as they don the thin, white Tyvek suits that cover them from neck to foot. This will be messy.

Then I remember the odor-blocking gel and offer some to both detectives, before smearing some on my upper lip—an excellent opportunity to see if this stuff really works.

I unzip a black heavy-duty body bag and lay it on the floor. Inside it I lay a plastic liner that should contain the majority of the juice and keep it from oozing out the zipper. My plan is to wrap the body in the bed sheet and then hoist the whole package into the plastic liner without sullying the body bag. Easier said than done.

With the help of the two bunny-suit-clad detectives, I slide Mr. Warner off the bed and attempt to gently lay him in the body bag. This proves to be problematic as Mr. Warner is just as heavy as he looks. With an unceremonious thud he stops short of the goal, dripping purge fluid on the outside of the body bag and liner. One of the detectives turns to gag, recomposes himself, and then continues the operation.

Ultimately, somehow, we get the solid portion of Mr. Warner into the bag and leave a large green and brown stain on the mattress. Since the ancient building's elevator doesn't accommodate a full-size gurney, we have to drag the body into it and sort of prop him up as he rides down to the lobby. There really is no suitable conversation that can be had between three sweaty people gathered around a decomposed body. "So, any plans for the weekend? How 'bout them Seahawks?" Doesn't happen. We ride in silence.

The wheeled cot, lowered to the ground, welcomes us in the lobby as the elevator's elderly door creaks open. We heft the body onto it and secure it with belts as tightly as possible. The last thing we need is for the body to fall off when the weight shifts. I walk ahead, carrying my camera kit, and the detectives wheel the gurney.

Ahead of us, the door to the stairway swings open and a rail-thin woman, plaid button-up hanging off her spare frame, breezes through. On her face is written the traces of a hard life. Between her spindly fingers she carries an unlit cigarette. She glances briefly at us and then heads towards the front door. "Blaah!" she says, and fans the air in front of her. "Smells like something died in here!" Never mind the three sweaty, biohazard-suited guys or, for that matter, the inert black lump being wheeled down the hallway. I wonder about some folks' powers of observation.

Into the cold, dry winter day we go, our silent companion creaking along on his extra-wide mortuary cot. I load him, the camera kit, and his property into the green van, and shut the double doors. The detectives doff their suits as quickly as they can, as if they are toxic.

"So," I say, "did that odor-blocking gel work?"

"Not really," says one of the detectives.

I drive five minutes to the morgue, located at the back side of Skagit Valley Hospital, next to the dumpsters, biohazard bins, and a very attractive parking lot. I use my key card to enter, and wheel my cargo into the cavernous cooler, where another plastic-wrapped body already reposes, a casualty from the hospital, a woman who had died upstairs in the intensive care unit.

I slide the body onto a shelf, write his name on the dry-erase board, and shut the heavy insulated door. The odor, as tenacious as an annoying child, follows me into the adjoining room.

From the roll on the wall, I rip a plastic sheet to replenish my supply. On it I place the burgundy cot cover and snap the buckles. Ready for the next customer.

When I arrive at the office, I set to work on the mundane task of inventorying the dead man's property, which consists of a set of keys, a cell phone, and a thick black wallet that has, unfortunately, taken on the same putrid funk as the body itself. The wallet is stuffed with ragged little notes of little value, an identification card, and a few gift cards from Christmases past. There is no cash, and nothing leads me any closer to finding this person's next of kin.

I open the flip phone, nearly out of battery, and discover that the last call was on Christmas, a month prior, in which the decedent had placed a call to "Sisto." I imagined a small boy, unable to yet pronounce his "r's," referring to his older sibling as such. It humanized him really, made him more than a smelly and inconvenient lump I had to dispose of. He had a family, a childhood, and surely never meant to end up the way he did.

This "Sisto" was likely to be the man's nearest next of kin, but my satisfaction at finding what was likely to lead me closer to closing the case was tempered by the trepidation always inherent in a death notification. As I had so many times, I was about to drop the worst news on an unsuspecting person.

I rehearsed my lines, found a scrap of paper to scribble notes on, opened my own phone, took a deep breath, and dialed...

The phone rang several times. I hoped a message would come on and I would be "off the hook" for the evening. Tomorrow, the duty investigator would get to "drop the bomb." But then, a voice.

"Hello?"

"My name is Matthew and I work for the County."

"Yes?"

"Do you know Scott Warner?"

"Yes, he's my brother."

*Deep breath.* "I am afraid I have some very bad news. Scott was found dead."

A brief pause. "What happened?"

"It's likely he died as a result of his alcohol problems."

A longer pause and a sigh. "Well, what should I do now?"

I explain the need for his physician to sign a death certificate and for her to choose a funeral home. I brief her on the contents of his apartment and the few belongings I am securing at the office. She agrees to pick them up the following week.

"I always knew this day would come," she says. "He struggled for so long."

I imagined a day in late December, maybe Christmas day, when Scott, feeling ill perhaps, took to his bed. Since he didn't appear to be tucked in for the night, maybe he thought he would just rest a while until the unpleasant feeling passed. Eventually the processes that had been eroding his body for so long reached their conclusion and his heart

79

shuddered to a stop.

As the hours turned into days, and the days turned into weeks, his body remained still, but changed nonetheless, his skin turning from white to green, darkening until it was black. He began to stink. His fingers and toes shriveled as his belly bloated with gas. His skin formed blisters and separated from the tissue underneath. The stench increased to the point where it seemed hard to believe that nobody noticed. Tenants in the building walked back and forth from their apartments, separated only by wood and plaster, apparently blissfully ignorant of the rotting corpse mere feet away. Maybe an unusual odor wafted out from time to time and was dismissed as poor housekeeping or food left out for too long.

Each morning the sun rose, casting its rays through Scott's dirty window and onto his rapidly changing corpse. Each evening as the sun slipped beyond the horizon, the light faded but the process in Scott's body continued undaunted, accompanied by a softly playing radio and dimly lit by a tiny lamp. Autolysis and bacterial decay worked in harmony to reduce what was once living into the raw material of something new. *And nobody noticed.*

Nobody noticed that he hadn't left his apartment in a month. Nobody cared enough to investigate the reason he hadn't shown up to his doctor's appointment. No supervisor missed him at work. He had no job. If he had friends, nobody stopped by to see him. *For a month.*

I thought of my own life, how many obligations I have, places I need to be, and people who rely on me. This man had no one. Nobody missed him.

The following day I phoned his physician, who hadn't seen him in some time, so I agreed to sign the death certificate. His belongings were picked up, and my report was completed. The case was closed.

Now it was up to the apartment manager to arrange for his

apartment to be thoroughly cleaned, the mattress disposed of, and the carpets to be shampooed. What little possessions he had were moved out and donated to a charity. Scott's body was quickly cremated at a local funeral home and reduced to eight pounds of ash. Effectively, all traces of him had disappeared.

I put a new air freshener in my van, replaced the body bags, and readied it for the next case.

# Autopsy

Barbara hums as she guides the scalpel behind the ears of the vagrant unfortunate enough to end up on our stainless steel table this fine sunny day. Bloodlessly, the skin separates to reveal a hint of the galea aponeurotica, a band of connective tissue that cocoons the skull. Then, using short, deft movements of the scalpel's blade, she begins dissecting forward, towards the forehead, cleaving the scalp from its underpinnings.

"Always look on the bright side of life!" she sings—a line from the last song of Monty Python's "The Life of Brian" in which a prisoner croons from his wooden cross. She sings as though serenading the dead man's remains, imploring him to have a better day than the one that brought him to us.

The scalp is now folded down over the man's face, completely obscuring his features, a few straggly scalp hairs brushing his stubbly chin, beard-like; it is time for the bone saw. With one hand steadying the top of the skull, Barbara presses firmly in an imaginary line circumnavigating the top of the skull. The high-pitched whine of the reciprocating saw drowns out her humming, but I can still see that she is. Her eyes shine above her surgical mask.

Dark blood oozes out from the trench created by the saw blade. Much as sawdust falls to the sides of a chainsaw blade, bone dust forms and fills the room with its acrid odor.

The cut complete, Barbara lays down the saw and picks up a skull key, a metal device with a broad screwdriver-type tip that will be used to leverage the skull cap off the tough underlying dura mater.

"I've always got a song in my head," says Barbara. "Do you?"

I do, often an aggravatingly annoying one, such as "The Hamster Dance." I wake up with them, go to bed with them, and to my chagrin, I am unable to get rid of them. Sometimes these songs become audible as I accidentally burst into song, much to the puzzlement of those around me.

With a "thwuck" sound, the skull cap comes off and Barbara lays it upside down on the steel table. The dura mater, tough and beige, lies protectively over the delicate, gelatinous brain.

As Barbara removes the dura and thrusts her small hands into the cranium to sever the brain from its stem, her husband, Graham, a forensic pathologist, dissects the abdominal organs. The couple are an anomaly in the world of death and decay, two perpetually positive folks who welcome a rainstorm as joyfully as most people would welcome a warm, sunny day. Their voices are gentle and they remain respectful of the dead, regardless of the sordid details that may have led them to their demise.

Graham, a vegetarian, and Barbara, a vegan, are also tender souls when it comes to vermin in their own house. Instead of setting traps that snap the necks of mice or leave them to starve to death on a sticky trap, Graham traps them and drives them far from his home to release them into the wild. It is though his constant exposure to death has made the idea of killing even the smallest animal utterly repugnant to him.

Barbara cradles the newly released brain in her gloved hands, as gently as if it were a new baby. The seat of the soul, of fifty years of memories, joy and pain, the command center of this now destroyed human, looks terribly vulnerable and fragile, jiggling like gelatin as Barbara places it on a gray plastic board for photography.

I know little of the man whose nude and flayed-open remains repose on the cold autopsy table, only that he was found facedown in a friend's house after complaining of not feeling well. An alcoholic without a permanent residence, he was well known to the local police for sleeping off his stupors in the alleyways and parking lots of Mount Vernon. The clothes we had stripped off him prior to autopsy had been ragged, soiled, and stained with urine. After removing two shirts, we discovered tiny bugs that had made a home between the layers of clothing, lice perhaps, though Graham wasn't sure.

His skin is scabbed from itching, his toenails long and yellow. He had long ago given up on hygiene in favor of pursuing the next drink. We had rinsed and scrubbed the dirty skin and turned him this way and that to make note of his scars and multiple tattoos, the marks of a storied life that had ended way too soon.

I take digital photographs of the brain as it would appear looking downwards from the top of the head and then gently turn it over to photograph the underside. Visible are the cerebellum, the center of balance, as well as the pons and medulla, brain centers that control breathing, blood pressure, and such basic functions as yawning and blinking.

Graham has removed all the organs from the chest and belly and placed them in a shallow bucket. From here he will remove each, weigh and dissect them. The heart is much too large at 450 grams, floppy and soft from the effects of chronic alcoholism and high blood pressure. The liver, unnaturally yellow and spongy, its surface irregular, is proof of the alcoholic cirrhosis and Hepatitis C noted in the medical records on the desk beside the table.

However, it is the lungs that most interest the pathologist. As he slices through the delicate pulmonary tissue, he notes foam in the small airways, or bronchioles, that terminate in tiny air sacs, known as alveoli—evidence of pneumonia, not an uncommon occurrence in an individual as weakened as this man.

He takes tiny samples from each organ and places them in cases for further study under a microscope. The rest of the sliced organs he places in a plastic bag that lines a standard five-gallon bucket. Before concluding his examination, he slices the brain into sections, using a broad, non-serrated knife, making it appear not unlike he is preparing sushi. He notes no strokes or tumors, but the brain is smaller than it should be, owing to the tissue-shrinking effects of chronic alcohol intake.

Since it will be my responsibility to sign this man's death certificate, I need to be sure of the cause and manner of his death, as well as the time interval over which the effects occurred. There exist only five manners of death—natural, accidental, homicide, suicide, or undetermined, but potentially thousands of causes of death, some occurring in seconds, others taking many years to wreak their deadly effects.

The pathologist thinks aloud in his soft, monotone voice. "There are several conditions that could have caused this man's death. He's got cardiomyopathy, moderate stenosis of the coronary arteries, and a fatty liver, as well as the pneumonia, but I think given the circumstances of his death and his complaint of not feeling well over the course of a few hours, I'll say his cause of death is pneumonia, and we can list the heart and the liver as contributory. Does that sound right to you?"

I am flattered that he has considered my opinion in his determination, because I am all too aware that his medical knowledge and experience dwarfs mine several hundred-fold. However, I think it is a mark of a great physician when he can be humble and able to take into account viewpoints other than his own.

"Yes, that sounds about right," I say.

Often it is difficult to determine exactly what was directly responsible for someone's death at the exact time that it occurred. Since nobody was around to peer directly into the body as it was dying, all we have is a body with several things that do not appear quite right, any of which could potentially cause death. Except in cases of trauma, such as multiple gunshot wounds to the chest, or decapitation, an educated guess is made as to the cause of death, given multiple organ abnormalities, combined with the results of toxicology tests, the results of which may take weeks or even months to come in from the State Toxicology Lab. Such results can often change the cause of death, if, say, the decedent's alcohol level came back sky-high, or there were lethal levels of narcotics in the system.

By this time, Barbara has begun re-assembling the body as neatly as possible. "Do you know, Matt, will this be an embalming?" she asks.

"We don't have a funeral home designated yet, but I really doubt it."

Barbara nods. Regardless of the disposition of the body—cremation or burial, Barbara reconstructs the body with the utmost of care. She places the skull cap back on the empty skull and folds the scalp back into its original position. With tight sutures of heavy twine, she sutures the skin back into place so that the scalpel margins are almost imperceptible. The large plastic bag of organs is secured with a zip tie and placed in the canoe-like abdominopelvic cavity. Barbara replaces the breast plate and then begins tightly sewing together the skin flaps created by the y-incision.

After rinsing the blood off the man's skin, she shampoos and combs out his long, tangled, and sparsely distributed hair. She closes his eyes and he appears much more peaceful than when he came in, possibly more peaceful than he had appeared in years.

In autopsy, my colleagues and I are charged with a responsibility that is both awesome and humbling, writing the final chapter of someone's life. As we peel back the layers of skin to reveal the often-damaged organs within, we are figuratively peeling back layers of someone's life, less to reveal how they had died, but more to reveal how they had lived. I continue to be struck by how many meet their end through their own self-abuse or neglect, the years of imbibing, the unhealthy diets, a drug to get you up in the morning, and one to put you to bed, a never-ending cycle.

Before I started in the death-care industry, I had no conception of how many lives ended prematurely because of addictions, whether to food, alcohol, drugs, or cigarettes. When we open them up at autopsy, their innards look as rough as their graying skin and generally haggard appearance. Black-speckled lungs, arteries so hardened they make a "chink" sound when they are struck with a pair of forceps, massive, floppy, myopathic hearts rendered useless by high blood pressure or alcohol, and livers so shrunken and yellow they are only recognizable by their position within the abdominal cavity. If people could only see inside themselves to realize the damage they were doing, maybe they would stop. Then again, maybe they wouldn't. But it's all preventable. The sad fact that healthy bodies are destroyed every day by insidious, long-term poisoning from foreign substances is still something I find vexing.

As death investigators, we don't see the healthy ones, those who had lived to enjoy a long and happy retirement, those who passed peacefully in their beds at ninety years of life. We see those whose choices have led them to where they are, the one without hope who hangs himself from a rafter in a garage at twenty-five years old, the fifty-year-old woman who makes the fateful decision to drive after five martinis and wraps her car around a tree, the young methamphetamine addict who collapses into unconsciousness and chokes on his own vomit.

And when I meet their grieving families, I often get a glimpse into the conditions into which these dead folks may have been born. The apple doesn't fall far from the tree, so to speak. The wheezing mother of an alcoholic arriving at the office to pick up his personal belongings, appearing much older than the age her driver's license photo states, her world-weary face heavily lined, her fingertips brown with nicotine stains, coping with her own addictions, the meth'ed out thirty-year-old son fidgeting at the scene of his sixty-year-old father's demise from heroin after so many years of cheating death.

At least we are able to give families some answers as to the final days, hours, and minutes or their loved one's lives. "Closure" really never happens. The pain of loss fades somewhat with time, but never fully goes away. Months later, I have received phone calls from family members, wanting once again, to be very sure of the details of their loved one's death. Did he suffer? Was there a clue someone missed that could have prevented this? My answers are the same: No, he didn't suffer. It was very quick. No, there was nothing you could have done to prevent your daughter from fatally overdosing. To say anything different would invite the growing, gnawing sense of regret that makes us want to go back in time and change things, though of course we never can.

As Barbara slicks the last few wet strands of hair against the dead man's scalp, she once again begins to sing. "Always look on the bright side of death, hm hm. Hm hm hm hm hm hm. Just before you draw your terminal breath…"

# Lamentation on a Cheeseburger

As I inhale the last few bites of my second McDonald's double quarter-pounder with cheese, I contemplate the almost certain sad state of my coronary arteries. I imagine the pathologist pointing with his scalpel at a cross-section of my left anterior descending artery, plugged at 90%, allowing only a trickle of blood to pass through to my oxygen-starved heart. "Well, I think we have a cause of death," he says, rather matter-of-factly. Of course, then there is the extra-large portion of fat-saturated, over-salted fries still left on my greasy tray. Would I like to supersize that? Why, of course! Once again, my need for sustenance—any sustenance, has won out over my better judgment, bolstered by years of witnessing the ravages of heart disease, both as a paramedic treating chest pain patients, and as a deputy coroner, observing the end results of bad dietary choices.

Despite witnessing, on a daily basis, the devastating effects of un-natural "food" on the body, the ravages of chronic alcoholism, and the disintegration of the lung tissue by heavy smoking, those of us in the death business are not, on the whole, any healthier than those who aren't. Maybe it's difficult to believe that what has happened to so many others couldn't happen to us, or perhaps it's a more informed igno-rance—"yeah, this stuff will kill me someday, but I'm not about to quit." Everybody needs a fix. An embalmer I once worked with, as he exhaled nasally a goodly portion of acrid cigarette smoke stated, "I'm working on about three different types of cancer right now." To say nothing of the lung and throat cancer almost certainly stewing away in his respira-tory tract, he breathed in formaldehyde fumes from embalming, without a mask, in an unventilated room, increasing his risk for leukemia. As he stubbed out his cigarette, he said, "Well, I'm off to the Mexican restaurant for a drink." And off he went.

I recall the time I drove an ambulance into the covered parking area at a hospital emergency entrance in Tacoma and left the engine idling as my partner went inside for some supplies. An RN in scrubs stood just outside the automatic doors, puffing on a cigarette and fanning the air in an exaggerated manner in annoyance at our diesel fumes. God forbid that our fossil-fuel emissions should detract from the delicious taste of her carcinogen-laden cigs. I had glanced through the windshield with bemusement at this rather shriveled woman in blue scrubs, shrugged, and shut off the engine.

The death rate still stands at 100%. Always has, always will. The Grim Reaper will get us all in the end. Whether you drink wheat grass smoothies and run ten miles a day or live on junk food and contemplate your expanding belly, everyone who reads this, yours truly included, will be dead in eighty years or so. I've seen many a former resident of planet Earth who has eschewed any form of risky behavior and still ended up just as dead as the guy who jumped out of perfectly good airplanes and whizzed around on a motorcycle. The stress of working in a business that involves daily interactions with distraught families, persons both living and dead in various states of trauma and disrepair, and irregular hours can often give rise to the pursuit of any meal, no matter how unhealthy, nicotine to briefly energize, or alcohol to numb us to what we see every day.

Though the unhealthy habits that many of us in the death business have taken on may surprise the un-indoctrinated, we really aren't that different than the average Joe on the street. Morticians, death investigators, and pathologists don't appear any different than anyone else. With a few exceptions, the pale, ghoulish, hollow-eyed, and dour stereotype of a mortuary worker doesn't hold water. To the contrary, most are happy, full of humor, and often very involved in their families, churches, and communities.

While my dietary habits may leave much to be desired and alcohol is a frequent companion, I haven't given up entirely on my health. At forty years old, married to a younger woman, and with a brand-new baby daughter, I've decided that I'd like to spend a little more time above ground before I take The Big Snooze. I take fish oil, I floss, and I do calisthenics, much to the amusement of my little dog, who looks at me in puzzlement as I leap into the air with all the gracefulness of a rhinoceros attempting ballet. All these activities I have come to consider as very adult. As I notice the fine lines under my eyes in the mirror and experience the hesitancy and dribbling from an enlarged prostate, I am reminded of the passage of time, the unstoppable momentum of aging, and the inevitability of death.

# Breaking the News

Though it could certainly be argued that my compassion for animals has always exceeded my compassion for humans, there is one aspect of the job of deputy coroner that still makes my heart churn—death notifications, occasions when it is necessary to either make a phone call or travel to the residence of the identified next of kin and "drop the bomb," so to speak.

The first duty of a medicolegal death investigator is to identify the deceased, whether by comparison to a driver's license or mug shot photo, or by more advanced methods such as fingerprinting or dental record comparison. The second duty and, arguably, the most mentally and emotionally taxing, is the notification of next of kin. While many think the job of coroner is primarily as a body-snatcher, they don't seem to grasp that most of our work is done with the living. We have to be *de facto* grief counselors, as well as scientists. Fortunately, in our county, we have a cadre of individuals dedicated enough to volunteer to assist us in this task—the county Support Officers. Clergy, retired teachers, and volunteer firefighters make up their ranks. They usually arrive before us on scene, having been dispatched by fire personnel or police on scene with a death. They are instrumental in explaining to the family "what happens next" from the often-unpleasant process of body removal, to the selecting of a funeral home.

I never do a death notification alone. Families' reactions to the news of the death of their loved one range from numb silence to outright denial, to bizarre behavior, screaming, pounding of fists, death threats to the investigators, "killing the messenger" so to speak. It is also not a good idea to approach a residence, unarmed, at 2 a.m., by oneself, and knock on the door. People woken out of a dead sleep can be confused, scared, and arm themselves readily either with a bat, a crowbar, or a double-barreled shotgun. Also, some folks are just plain nuts. In order to prevent my career from being cut short in such a fashion, I will either be accompanied by a Support Officer or a member of law enforcement on every in-person death notification.

Nothing in my training has been adequate at preparing me for the reactions I get when I give the worst news. When I stand at the door and inform a mother and a father that their son has shot himself in the head, that he's never coming home again, that he will forever now be referred to in the past tense, I have delivered a crushing blow. With a few words, I have effectively just destroyed their world.

When I deliver the worst news, various reactions may occur, among them a shocked silence, weeping, sudden collapse, and spontaneous destruction of property. The worst though, is the death wail.

I will never forget the first time I heard it in the early morning hours of a foggy winter night in 1989. I was a volunteer firefighter and we had just concluded a valiant attempt at saving an elderly man's life. We had failed. As I stood in the darkness beside the ambulance, I heard the wail cut through the night, the most piercing, agonizing, hopeless sound I had ever heard. It seemed to tear into my solar plexus, then exit, removing a little bit of my soul as it left. The lead paramedic had just informed Cliff's wife that, after fifty years of marriage, he was no more.

Since that time, I've heard the death wail countless more times. I've had the sad duty to inform a young boy that his mother had overdosed and died—on his birthday of all times. The look of utter shock, the keening, the slow collapse to the floor, the primitive knowledge that life has forever changed…I have felt my mouth go dry and my heart beat in my throat as I spoke on the phone to a mother hundreds of miles away, telling her that her son had hanged himself. I know what is coming next.

As devoid as I feel of emotion at times, and as easily and nonchalantly as I am able to walk into a room full of flies and stinking of human decomposition, I will never be able to rid the death wail from my mind as long as I live.

On one of the last days of summer, with the chill of fall already in the air and the leaves beginning to turn, I heard the death wail again, but this time it came from my own throat. I stood over the tiny and lifeless body of my dog, killed at four years old by the neighbor's lab. "Not now. Not Micah," I had thought. The wail pervaded the neighborhood, and soon two neighbors came running. I didn't care who heard. He may have been "only" a dog, but he was better than most people I had met.

When I could wail no more for the loss of my friend, I sank to the grass, exhausted, and stroked his blood-streaked fur. I was no longer just the bearer of bad news. I was also its recipient. The sudden death of a loved one cuts us from the inside out and forces us to re-evaluate our priorities. Shortly after Micah's death, I began to think more seriously about my own mortality. Perhaps I don't have forty or fifty more years left on this planet. I may leave as quickly and as unexpectedly as Micah did, or as precipitously as the folks I zip into a plastic bag in the afternoon, when just that morning they had expected to live forever.

Rest well, little friend. I'll see you at the end of days.

But…in the midst of sorrow, there is always the promise of new life.

# Klaire

On a cold, gray January 27, at 0931 hours, my beautiful baby daughter Klaire was born and life was forever changed.

I was forty and had thought I would never have children. It just didn't seem to be in my nature. I had considered children an annoyance, a disruption of my peace—noisy, clumsy, dirty organisms who only bore a passing resemblance to adults. Even my own father disliked children, and does to this day. Shortly after he and my mother married, it became obvious that they had failed to have a very important pre-marital discussion on the subject of children. While my mother wanted kids, my father envisioned a future with small, furry, four-legged children. It seemed to be, in part, an attempt to recapture what he had lost as a youth. When he was young, his family had owned a beagle. One day, he had attempted to give her a bath. Apparently, the beagle had disliked this idea so much that she had run off, soapy water dripping off her, and was never seen again.

In the end, my mother had won, (obviously) and my father was either blessed or cursed with two boys. I was the oldest; my brother followed three years later. Though I had given both my parents innumerable headaches and sleepless nights, especially during my rebellious teenage years, my father does confess that I have made life "more interesting" for both he and my mother. "Without you guys, our lives would be boring," he had once said. I wasn't sure whether to take this as a compliment or not.

Long before there was Klaire, there was Micah, the little Yorkshire terrier my wife and I had adopted as a couple three years prior. I had never been a "dog person." I thought they resembled children in that they seemed overly friendly, smelled bad, and would jump on people when they least expected it. They were fine in theory, as long as I wasn't slobbered on. But Kenzie wanted a dog, and she wouldn't give up until we had the small, furry bundle in our arms.

She did internet searches for Yorkie puppies deep into the night while I lamented the responsibility of caring for a dog. I issued such bright-line imperatives as "the dog will not be allowed in or on the bed" and "the dog will be your responsibility." At the time, Micah was just "the dog," devoid of personality or even gender.

When we finally found a breeder that we felt fairly confident wasn't going to swindle us out of our money, we traveled to the breeder's home to select a puppy. A new litter of Yorkies had been born as well as a new litter of YorkiePoos—a blend of Yorkie and Poodle. While Kenzie oohed and aahed over the YorkiePoos, I thrust my hand into the wriggling mass of tiny newborn Yorkies in the cardboard box and pulled out the second-smallest, a little runt that was trying to nurse but kept getting trampled by the bigger puppies. I held him up, proclaimed him "The One," and the rest, as they say, is history.

When he arrived home that night, Kenzie and I wrapped him up in much the same way as a newborn human baby would be swaddled, gazed adoringly on his fuzzy countenance, and put him to bed. He cried all night.

It was then that I felt the first real stirrings of affection for the little creature. Here was an animal that missed his litter-mates and depended on us for every aspect of his survival. Within weeks, my hard-nosed approach to dog parenting disintegrated entirely. I became Micah's playmate, his janitor, and his waiter, making sure he always had clean food and enough water.

"The dog will not be allowed in or on the bed" became "Sneak

Micah into the bed, give him his own little blanket, and let him sleep beside me all night." I had become a sucker.

So it was of no surprise that when we welcomed Klaire into our lives, I would fall in love with her as well.

Klaire decided to make her grand entrance onto the stage of life through a window instead of a door. Dressed in surgical garb, I held Kenzie's hand as four doctors and as many nurses pulled and prodded our little progeny through an abdominal incision and into a bright, cold world.

I watched helplessly as the pediatrician and her staff dried and stimulated a limp and blue Klaire, attaching an oxygen mask onto her tiny face, and slapping EKG electrodes on her chest. It was a Caesarean Section like so many others that, I am sure, took place across the nation that day, routine as morning coffee for the hospital staff, but extraordinary for me. Etched indelibly in my memory of that day was, in a scene reminiscent of Michelangelo's Creation of Man on the ceiling of the Sistine Chapel, Kenzie reaching out and being able to briefly touch the hand of her newborn before she was whisked away to the nursery.

Within a few minutes, Klaire's dusky blue fingers and toes turned to a more reassuring pink, and she screeched her lungs out, announcing her triumphant debut as planet Earth's newest citizen.

She was beautiful and perfect and a miracle. As a man of science, with a degree in Human Biology, I understand embryology and human development pretty well, so I don't toss out the term "miracle" in a cavalier fashion. How lucky were we!

The birth of my daughter was also the first glimpse I had of my own mortality. Klaire was my legacy, the progenitor of all future generations to replace me. This wiggling, pink little being was to become the gray-haired woman who, many years in the future (I hope) would sit at my bedside during my last days. Having a child forced me to acknowledge the fact that life is astonishingly short. As we parents begin our inevitable physiological decline with slowing metabolism and its attendant weight gain around the middle, the sagging flesh, the graying hair, those who are to survive us are just beginning their evolution into fully formed human beings.

Klaire's birth brought other feelings I had never expected. I'd always been ambivalent about children, though I had little experience dealing with their premature deaths. A couple of months later, my wife and I were driving in Northern California, on vacation, far away from work, when a vivid image flashed into my head—that of a young father lowering his infant son's tiny white casket into a shallow grave. I had been one of two funeral directors leading the service of a baby who had died shortly after birth. I looked back at my own child, snoozing peacefully in her car seat, and my eyes filled with tears, the first tears I can remember shedding for the death of a child. In this child's death, the natural order of things had been fractured, palpably so, and it had meant nothing to me until Klaire had awakened in me a long-dormant or long-suppressed paternal instinct. As never before, I had the need to protect, to walk through fire if it was necessary, my daughter, my bloodline, my DNA.

Moreover, with Klaire's birth, I realized that every life decision I had made, every job I had lost, whether by my own stupidity or other circumstances, and every relationship that didn't work had led me to this beautiful place. Were it not for every nuance, every turn in my life's path, she wouldn't be here.

That night, I put Klaire down in her little fold-up crib next to our bed at the in-laws' house. I kissed her forehead and hoped a million things for her future. At two and a half months old, it was the first time she had ever slept through the night.

# River Body

"Why would you do this job?" asks the deputy sheriff, with a mixture of incredulity and disgust.

"Somebody has to," I reply. "Why not me?"

He's piloting the inflatable County Sheriff boat up the Skagit River as I shiver in the bow in my shirtsleeves, ill-prepared for the brisk late October weather.

The deputy is persistent. "Why would *anyone* do this job?"

"I enjoy it," I say simply.

The other deputy relaxes in the stern as we motor out to a sandbar, where I am told, a dead body lies, and has been lying for some time. The trip is taking a while.

"How bad is he?" I ask.

"Like a dead seal," he replies. "All bloated up...stinks."

I had parked my Green Van O'Death at a fairly remote boat launch about forty minutes east of our office in Mount Vernon. The detective I had spoken to had asked me to bring "a lot of equipment," whatever that meant. Was he in pieces? Did I need a separate little bag for each body part? And what kind of equipment did he think I had? Other than a body bag or two, a stretcher, and a full tank of gas, I didn't have much.

The victim, I had been told, had been missing for three months and presumed dead, after falling out of his boat in a state of intoxication. In July, witnesses had reported seeing a man falling out of his boat and subsequently flailing in the water before disappearing as his boat, unmanned, went around in circles nearby. He had been reported missing by his wife shortly thereafter, and she had provided, in the missing person report, a description of a distinctive tattoo on the gentleman's right forearm.

The deputy cuts the motor and the boat drifts to a stop on the rocky shore. I bring with me a bright orange water recovery bag, basically a mesh bag with a zipper that would allow us to strain the water out of a corpse as we lift it into a boat. Additionally, I bring a light, zippered body pouch, of the style used in hospitals, to contain as much of the "juice" as possible. Bodies leaking all over my van are not my cup of tea.

A third deputy stands ashore a short distance away. When we approach, he points in the direction of a tangle of downed trees that could have been a logjam had the river been higher. Amidst the scatter of tree limbs is barely visible a still figure, gray as molding clay, partially hidden by a large tree trunk. I approach, snapping photos as I go.

What remains of the man we believe is Neal Backman is at once both pitiful and terrifying. He is terrifying in that he resembles the best of a Hollywood make-up artist's attempts to create a zombie, gray skin hanging in shreds, ribs visible, facial features distorted and sloughing off. Pitiful in that as he lies on his left side, his left arm outstretched, it is as though he is grasping for a life ring that never arrives.

Oddly enough, in three months of bobbing about underwater and being caught in various eddies, currents, and log-jams, he still wears a pair of cargo shorts of an indeterminate color, and his wristwatch still gleams on his left wrist. A gold chain adorns his neck, contrasting with his unnaturally gray skin tone. His chest is split open mid-sternum, which I assume is an open-heart surgery scar that had come undone as his body disintegrated, and through it I can glimpse his shriveled heart. His tattoo is still legible on his forearm.

"How do you want to do this?" asks one of the deputies.

"Well," I say. "You grab a leg and I'll grab an arm and we'll scoot him on over to this bag."

"What if his arm falls off?" asks the deputy.

I shrug.

"I'll hold your camera for you," says the deputy.

The arm stays intact, as does the rest of him, and within a few minutes we have the sodden remains enclosed in a thin white zippered body bag and make our way along the rocky beach back to the waiting boat. It is at this auspicious moment that the deputy actually uses the camera. "This would be a great picture for the Christmas party," he says. I'm glad he's found something positive about the whole situation.

Through the choppy water we go, our decomposed cargo in the bow, back to the dock. The pre-attached identification tag flaps in the breeze. The putrescent stench of decay is replaced by the aroma of mud, trees, and burnt fuel.

Once the body is secured on the cot and in the van, the smell, for so long dissipated by ambient air, reaches out with a vengeance. Like a living thing, it creeps through the partial partition and invades the driver's compartment. I roll both windows down and set course for the morgue. I wish I had a cigar. I am reminded of a case I did years ago when I volunteered for another Coroner's Office. My partner, Rico, and I had a badly decomposed alcoholic in the back, which seemed to smell worse than a "standard" decomp. Rats had been munching away on his hands and face for several days. Rico had brought along two large stogies, and we had cruised, windows down, cigar smoke billowing, on a sunny day, past motorists and pedestrians, who, for all they knew, were witnessing two golf buddies, on their way home from the bar, enjoying the evening. The van was unmarked, allowing us to travel in relative obscurity, to and from our morbid destinations.

A light rain sprinkles the asphalt as I back the green van into the parking lot outside the morgue. I can't smell the body anymore, due to olfactory overload, but what I can smell is the dumpster outside the morgue entrance, hardly an improvement.

I pull the cot out and the two sets of wheels extend and automatically lock in place. With my ID badge, I open the secured door and wheel my cargo into the morgue anteroom. It's a sparsely furnished and silent place. A walk-in cooler, set at a constant 42 degrees F, hums in the corner. A desk is situated near a door that opens to the greater hospital, next to a folded-up reserve removal cot and a covered hospital gurney, used to remove bodies from the various floors of the hospital. Adjacent to the morgue anteroom is the autopsy suite, a cramped space that reminds me of the funeral home embalming room in which I used to work. The ubiquitous smell of disinfectant fills the air, certainly preferable to the decomp stench I bring with me.

Since I need to check the body for identifying marks, I open the bag under brilliant florescent lights. Marinating in a broth of foul seawater, the remains are more pungent now at room temperature. I snap a photograph or two of the tattoo and then steel myself for the task ahead—plunging my gloved hands into the man's pockets in search of a wallet.

While the job of securing valuables is a necessary one, I always feel a bit intrusive as I'm rifling through pockets and removing rings and watches, as if the dead are watching me, perhaps with disgust, as though I were a thief. My hands reach into the soaked denim rear pocket and pluck a waterlogged black wallet. In it are a driver's license and the usual credit cards and business cards. These I will inventory at the office. A photograph of a beaming small child (maybe his son?) is remarkably well-preserved after three months underwater. I set it aside to dry before putting in storage. The man's wife will undoubtedly want to have it back.

I re-wrap the body in plastic and then, using a tape dispenser, secure the body with swathes of wide clear tape, as though I am wrapping a present—a very smelly present. Then, with a Sharpie, I write the man's name, our case number, and the date on the outside of the bag. I wheel him into the cooler and slide him over to a shelf, awaiting autopsy in the morning.

# The Hoarder

A large green lump lies before me on the sticky linoleum, taking up the majority of the bathroom, overflowing into the dirty bathtub, abutting the baseboard, and flowing semi-solidly around the commode. My eyes train downwards, towards my steel-toed boots and focus on a pair of bare purple feet, soles pointed skyward. I turn back to the threshold, where my father-in-law stares, in disbelief.

"How are you going to do this?" he asks.

Honestly, I have no idea. Yet, *I have no idea* isn't a viable answer. I am charged with removing dead bodies, no matter the size, and safely getting them to their ultimate destination.

"Well…"

The paramedic who had been on scene had sent me a cheery text message prior to my arrival: "Five hundred pounds. She's a hoarder. Good luck!" Jay, the other guy on the medic truck, had recommended a Viking Funeral.

I reach out with a gloved hand and pull back the green bath towel that covers the body. What greets me nearly makes me gasp out loud. Before me lies five hundred pounds of dead female humanity, facedown, a flimsy slip pulled up to her chest and underwear pulled to mid-thigh. Otherwise, she is naked.

I make my way to the door, kicking boxes filled with more boxes, defunct appliances, and a litter box to the side.

"Dispatch the fire department," I shout to the deputy sheriff who is waiting, safely, in the dreary drizzle outside. I'll need as much help as I can get.

My father-in-law, Lennie, and I clear debris out of the bathroom, tossing objects into the living room as though it were a dumpster, as we hear sirens wail in the night. The fire department has decided to respond rapidly to our call for assistance.

Within minutes, a fire engine and fire department Suburban arrive on scene, red lights twirling. Aside from the gray-haired, gray-mustached volunteer who arrives first in the suburban, the fire crew appears to be composed entirely of kids, their skinny teenage bodies draped in traditional school-bus yellow firefighting gear.

Like a flock of oversized ducklings, they crowd into the already cluttered entry area of the house, awaiting my instruction.

I stand in the bathroom once again and contemplate my upcoming task. Though the woman's size is daunting from the chest up, it is her lower extremities that are truly impressive. Her buttocks span four feet at least, and each one of her legs is twice the circumference of my own torso.

I turn to one of the tiny firemen. "You got a sheet?"

The fireman leaves and returns from his rig with a bed sheet. I step into the bathtub and shimmy it underneath her chest. My father-in-law and I each grab an end of the sheet and flop the top half of the woman onto the bathroom floor. Then Lennie and I puff, hands on our knees, sweat pouring off our foreheads, and plan our next move. This promises to be a long night.

I consider the mountain of humanity before me and imagine this must be what it's like to move dead livestock. Just when I begin to consider this an apt analogy, I am reminded that when an animal dies on a ranch, the rancher responsible for removal has considerably more room to work. Maybe if this were a pen of sorts?

105

"I need a hose strap," I gasp. One of the small and overly energetic young volunteers darts out the door, making a beeline for the truck, pausing only briefly to trip over a litter box and a phone book from ten years ago.

When the fireman returns, I slide the hose strap, designed to allow an average-sized firefighter to control a high-powered hose line, down the woman's torso and settle it underneath her ample belly. Next, we employ two more sheets, one around each thigh, and prepare to pull.

She budges six inches.

Again.

Maybe three this time.

*What if we can't move her? Will we need to remove the side of the house?* Embarrassing for me but humiliating for the family. Maybe Jay's idea of a Viking Funeral wasn't such a bad idea. What's Eating Gilbert Grape, Part II.

Another mighty pull from the gang and her feet are in the hallway. Another break to regain composure. Another pause to toss garbage out of our way and clear a path.

And she's still facedown, leaving a trail of bloody drool from the tub across the bathroom floor.

"We'll get her moved into the living room where there's more space," I say, "and then we'll turn her onto her back."

A fan, perched on a straight-back chair, blows lukewarm air into what had once been a living room, but now resembles a half-filled dumpster. An old tube-style television blares in the corner, entertaining the garbage. A house of despair. There are no functioning lights. All work is done by flashlight.

How did she come to this—this immense body? This domestic disaster? Like a mountain of debt or a failing relationship whose apathy has overcome its passion, I suspect it didn't happen overnight. This poor woman didn't just wake up one day in a pigsty, look at herself in the mirror, and say, "I am really large and really depressed." She was likely resigned to her fate of dying before her time, obese, lonely, and apathetic.

My feelings for this poor soul before me are a mixture of pity and contempt; pity for a human being who had lived such a sad existence, and contempt for one who had let her health suffer to such an extent that, in death, she has endangered the backs and knees of those responders who happened to be on duty when she met her end.

After much jostling, grunting, straining, sweating, and swearing, we manage to move our hapless cargo to what resembles the living room and flip her onto her back. She issues a guttural groan accompanied by a whiff of sulfurous air as the last of the final breath she ever took escapes into the room. By the yellowed beam of the fire department's battle lantern, I perform my forensic examination. Her face is deeply purple and congested with blood that has settled where gravity has commanded it to. The woman's eyes are swollen shut. I peel the lids back to reveal the whites of her eyes turned blood-red, hemorrhaged by gravity and the effects of early decomposition. Her teeth and tongue are caked with clotted blood, giving her a rather vampire-like appearance. Her chest is dotted with purple spots—small hemorrhages under the skin known as Tardieu spots. I palpate her head, feeling for depressions in her skull. Moving on to her neck, I check for signs of strangulation, marks on the neck or obvious crushing of the larynx. I find none. I check both hands for jewelry and photograph them. If the family were to claim that she was or wasn't wearing a particular item of jewelry, we would have photographic evidence to support our written report.

This is a job for our new device, the venerable Med Sled, a sort of extra-large toboggan for dead people composed of flexible plastic that, when secured with straps, envelops the body, compacting fat and distributing weight, making it much easier to move a heavy body down stairs and around tight corners. My boss had bought the device with surplus funds the previous year, anticipating this sort of scenario.

I place a sheet of blue plastic beneath the body before I secure it to the Med Sled—not just any sheet of plastic, but a heavy-duty sheet designed for those who exceed three hundred pounds. After wrapping the body with said plastic sheet, I secure the Med Sled around her, and suddenly she doesn't seem so intimidating, simply becoming a giant plastic burrito, as innocuous as any piece of furniture. An added bonus to the Med Sled is the extra-long handles, allowing a person to keep his back straight while dragging the laden device.

While I have been wrestling the device around the body, another volunteer firefighter has facilitated our exit by sawing the railing off the very small front porch—certainly preferable to removing an entire wall.

From here, the firefighters slide the body out of the living room, down the filthy hallway from whence we came, off the deck, and onto the extra-wide gurney, rated to one thousand pounds, that they had placed to the side of the deck. They then push the laden gurney across the muddy front lawn, and, with a mighty shove, place her in the back of my van.

Before leaving, I speak to her brother, who had called in the death. I confirm with him that she didn't have a doctor and didn't have any medical history and inform him that we will need to do an autopsy to determine a cause of death.

With Lennie in the passenger's seat, I drive to Kern Funeral Home. The coroner's morgue is too small to accommodate a person of her size. Her anterior/posterior dimensions will not allow her to fit on a shelf and there is no way of lifting her safely from cot to autopsy table and back. Kern Funeral Home has what amounts to a ceiling-mounted crane that allows for easy transfer.

The embalmer meets us at the funeral home and opens the garage door for us. We wheel the body in and help place her in the cooler, leaving her on the Med Sled for easy transfer later.

# Suicide

The yellowed beam of my flashlight hits the semi-prone figure in the gravel, illuminating jeans, tennis shoes, a heavy parka, and a tangled mass of hair obscuring a face of indeterminate gender. A small, congealed mass of blood stains the gravel to the side of the face, accented by bloody bubbles. I train the flashlight to all points of the compass around the corpse, looking for additional evidence and familiarizing myself with the area. Drops of blood are visible in the gravel a few feet away, leading to the body. The gravel is disturbed. The soles of the tennis shoes are bloody. I start shooting photos. My breath fogs the lens.

I'd gotten the call from the Sheriff's office—a suicide at Mile Marker 280 at a roadside turn off. A suicide note had been found at a local laundromat. The deputy tells me that the handwriting matches scribbled notes found inside the decedent's vehicle. The trip from my house had taken about an hour, from the bright lights of suburbia through the darkness, through the seemingly endless gentle curves of a two-lane road, flanked by grand old Douglas fir trees. Though my back ached as it always does when I'm in my seat too long, I hadn't minded too much. I had my iTunes, my coffee, and the heater going full blast.

Deputy Wright sits in his SUV on the street, out of the cold, illuminated by the bluish glow of his mobile data terminal, his engine idling. Deputy Scott, who has parked his car just ahead of my green van in the turnout, hands me the ID he has found in the dead person's car. The dead person is Linda Torelli, aged fifty-four years, from Arlington, Washington.

Jim's Towing's wrecker idles on the roadway. It seems to me a bit premature, considering I've just arrived on scene to investigate Linda's death, and the driver is intent on impounding her car. Life moves on, and very quickly.

I put my camera back in its yellow kit and retrieve my gurney from the van. After positioning it parallel to the body, I unfold the white plastic sheet and place it beside the body in preparation for rolling her onto it.

With blue-gloved hands, I grasp the dead woman's right arm, already stiffened from rigor mortis. I flip her onto her back. Steam rises from her mouth as the last of her body heat escapes. I shine my flashlight around again. A firearm is revealed. Underneath the rigored body is a black semi-automatic pistol, a .22 caliber. I shine my flashlight on her bloodied face and then to the photo of the driver's license found in the car. It's a match. I had thought at first that my victim was a man. She is a rather unfortunate-looking woman.

Deputy Scott shines his beam down on the gaping, bloody mouth and then at the blood-fouled firearm.

"Shot herself in the mouth, didn't she?"

"Don't know yet," I say.

Her sweatshirt is stained crimson down the entire front. I pull it upwards, towards her chin, to examine for underlying injuries. Just above her left breast is a dime-sized hole, still seeping blood. About two inches above that, another.

"Shot twice," I say.

Deputy Scott groans. "That's a problem."

While it is entirely possible for a person to shoot herself twice in the act of suicide, it is a little unusual and cause for some further investigation.

"Do you want me to hold off?" I say.

"Yeah. Let me get ahold of the on-call," says Deputy Scott. He goes back to his car to call the on-call detective.

Deputy Wright saunters over. "What's with the bubbles coming out of her mouth?" he asks.

"Well," I say. "Looks like she got herself in the lung at first. That explains the bubbles—air mixed with blood. The bottoms of her shoes have blood on them, so she must have walked a few paces with blood streaming down her legs and onto her shoes. Then she fired again and hit her heart—the fatal shot."

"Wow," says Deputy Wright. "I'm glad you're here."

Deputy Scott walks back over. "I'm getting the go-ahead. Detective doesn't want to come out. Clear case of suicide."

I continue my examination to include her hands, stiffened and blood-caked. I turn her pockets inside out—no papers or money to return to the next of kin.

After placing an ankle tag on the body, I wrap her in the plastic and place her on the gurney. After placing her in the van, I back out and, on cue, the tow truck backs in.

Once I'm on the way back to the morgue, I phone our forensic pathologist for a consultation. I can't imagine much would be gained by an autopsy, but, given the unusual circumstances, I'd like his opinion.

"I can feel the round through the skin on her back," I say. The bullet had just enough momentum to traverse the distance of her chest cavity, but not quite enough to penetrate the skin of her back and exit.

My plan is to take X-rays from two different angles to determine the trajectory of the bullet as sort of a virtual autopsy.

The pathologist agrees. "You can use a scalpel to remove the bullet from underneath her skin. That's not considered practicing medicine without a license."

When I arrive at the morgue, I unwrap the body and am able to better see her under the bright, glaring fluorescent lights. I turn her to her side and make an incision just above the bullet. I then squeeze the deformed round out and plop it into a specimen cup. It makes a metallic rattle. Monday, I will transfer the bullet to the Sheriff's Office. There it will remain for eternity, only to reappear if the family calls the death into question.

Unused evidence and unclaimed urns—kept in the musty back rooms and storage cabinets of funeral homes, sheriff's offices, and medical examiner's headquarters, unlikely to ever again see the light of day, but impossible to dispose of. Who would have use for a bullet used in the commission of a suicide? And who would come to claim an urn after it sits, unclaimed, for five years? The mortal, finely crushed remains of a loner, encased in a dusty, temporary urn, reposing silently on a shelf, will likely never be claimed by a family member. *But what if someone does?*

# Unique Families

I find it rather inconceivable that a man could fail to realize that his wife is dead...for three days.

I'd gotten the call early one morning from the Anacortes Police. An officer was on scene with a confirmed DOA. A fifty-six-year-old woman had been found dead in bed, her little dog snoozing beside her. Her husband had told the officer that he had last seen his wife—alive presumably—the previous night, though I knew better than to presume.

When he found her, he had started CPR on her and continued until paramedics arrived. They had quickly determined that the woman was beyond help and elected not to continue efforts.

I asked the officer if the dead woman had been ill, if she took any medications, or if she had a physician. The answer was no to all three of the questions, putting it into the category of a jurisdictional death—one that required further investigation, up to and possibly including an autopsy. The husband had mentioned something about alcohol and sleeping pills, so I assigned a case number and made arrangements for the body to be removed.

As I had care of our infant daughter, I wasn't able to respond to the scene, so I requested a funeral home on a rotational basis to make the removal.

Hawthorne Funeral Home sent their van out to the house and brought the body into their facility, where I'd scheduled an autopsy to take place the next morning.

When the pathologist and his assistant arrive, I begin to unzip the body bag to reveal the green face of a woman who has clearly been dead for more than just overnight. Dark fluid dribbles from her half-gaping mouth. As the zipper continues southward, the picture gets even more interesting. The woman's chest, bared, with a T-shirt pushed upwards, is crisscrossed with the lurid arboreal pattern of marbling, dark discolorations that follow the distribution of the veins, indicative of decomposition. The skin on her sternum is sloughing off where her husband had attempted CPR. The skin on both arms is also sloughing. This woman has been dead for at least two days.

The autopsy is fairly inconclusive and our determination of the cause of death will rely heavily on the results of toxicology. The funeral home has brought in a few empty blister packs of Carisoprodol, a sleeping medication.

When I phone the dead woman's husband to inform him of the results, or lack thereof, of our autopsy, I am anxious to hear the story behind her demise and delayed discovery.

I introduce myself and tell him that we would need to wait for toxicology results to arrive in four to six weeks to determine cause of death.

"We have a discrepancy," I say, "between your account of when she was last seen alive, and what we found at autopsy."

"How so?"

"Well, her face was green, and that indicates that she had been dead for some time."

"It was green?"

"Yes, and also her skin was beginning to slough off."

There is silence on the line.

"We sleep in separate bedrooms," he says. "She's an alcoholic, stays up late at night and then sleeps all day sometimes. She'd drink on the weekends, but didn't want to drink on weekdays, so she'd take those sleeping pills."

"I see."

"But we have a good marriage," he says, as though trying to convince me that his marriage was as normal as anyone else's. "I go to her room, or she goes to mine…"

He continues, "I came home from work the previous night and she was sleeping there, with the little dog beside her. So, I figured she was tired. I just let her sleep."

"Are you sure she was sleeping?"

"Well, I figured if something was wrong, the dog would let me know!"

I try to puzzle through how a dog would communicate that its master is dead. Certainly it wouldn't wag its tail? Would it whine, bark, chew on itself? I have no idea.

"She was very likely already dead that evening, sir," I say.

Reality begins, very slowly, to dawn on the gentleman. "Huh," he says, chewing on the revelation. "Come to think of it, I'm not sure if I talked to her the night before that either. Tuesday. That's it. I think I spoke to her Tuesday."

Three days prior. That would explain the degree of decomposition we saw at autopsy.

"I think it's likely she overdosed on sleeping pills, or alcohol, or a combination of the two," I say. "We'll probably never know exactly when she took them though."

The husband thanks me and hangs up. I sit at my desk and try to figure out how to word my corrected report. And then I imagine the husband, sitting, newly alone in a house suddenly much bigger and quieter than before, phone in hand, staring out the window at the noonday sun, trying to rationalize how he could have mistaken something as basic as the demise of his wife for sleep. Maybe he wonders if he could have done something sooner she might still be alive.

If there's anything the death profession has taught me, or for that matter, emergency medical services, is that one of the biggest fallacies is to assume that not only do other people think like you, but also that they will conduct their lives in a manner similar to yours. The definition of "normal" in a marriage varies immensely, from the stereotypical "happy" couple who see one another every evening and on the weekends, to those who are merely roommates, or who might maintain separate residences, or who may even maintain another relationship on the side.

Through the unique window into the lives of the deceased that death care provides me, I'm able to expand my perspective of what constitutes "normal" and "functional." What is normal to some is highly dysfunctional to another. Even the prototypical "Leave it to Beaver" family may seem bizarre to others who have grown up in a completely different way.

I recall a case in which I investigated the death of a middle-aged woman who was watching television with her husband when she suddenly began vomiting a dark fluid, became unresponsive, and died. An image came into my head as I made my way to the call—a neatly maintained living room, much like my own, freshly vacuumed carpet, a newly polished coffee table with perhaps a book or two on top, and the dead woman, lying on the carpet, with maybe a small amount of dark vomit beside her head.

What greeted me as I walked in the door of that house I couldn't have imagined. A wheelbarrow full of yard debris was actually parked in what had once been a kitchen. Dried marijuana buds sat atop a formerly white refrigerator and atop an island among crushed cans of cheap beer and the dried remnants of microwaveable dinners. Dishes that had been sitting in the sink so long they had developed several different species of greenish mold overflowed onto a counter whose former color was unidentifiable.

The dead woman herself, the subject of the investigation, was obese, nude, and lying on muddy composite flooring, smeared with dark bloody fluid. A couch, varnished with the sheen of years of body oils, hulked in the corner among the cobwebs. A urine stain marked where the woman had sat when she had breathed her last.

In my efforts to appreciate the decedent in situ, in her natural environment, my gaze fell upon the ceiling of what had once passed for a dining room. It didn't exist, exactly. A massive crater, flanked by chunks of drywall, loomed above a dusty table. Clear plastic sheeting, an apparent attempt at a temporary repair, ballooned with the burden of an entire season of rainwater, hung low over the table like a burgeoning aneurysm.

When we went to perform an autopsy on the woman the next day, we found that the condition of her internal organs reflected the condition of her house—decaying, neglected, and abused. Her brain was atrophied from alcoholism; her liver, instead of being red and resilient, was yellow and spongy—a fatty liver, from poor diet and alcohol. Her heart, a floppy, misshapen bag of blood, was the result of years of high blood pressure and alcohol. Most striking of all were her kidneys, which resembled no kidneys I had ever before seen: gray, granular, and amorphous. It wasn't possible to tell the right from the left.

This was her normal. I imagined the unfortunate woman, waking around noon and nursing a hangover with the hair of the dog, possibly wolfing down a stale burger from McDonald's around two; the kitchen was impossible to cook in. Then it was time for a nap, followed by an afternoon and evening of watching television on a couch likely crawling with so many micro-organisms it would cause my bacteriophobic wife to become apoplectic.

And so back home I go to my neat and organized house, leaving my stinking clothes in the garage—both a spatial and psychological distance I put between myself and my work. And though my bed is unmade and my bills are unpaid, strewn about my desk, I appreciate what I have just a little bit more.

# A Good Man

When I receive the call to investigate the death of Mr. Charles Rounds of 12256 Rounds Road, I am not even sure if his death is in our jurisdiction.

"Darrington? Is that even in Skagit County?"

"Yes," the 911 dispatcher replies. "Deputy Campbell is on scene."

That's a familiar name, so I suppose the deceased gentleman lived in one of those odd areas in which a town is split between two different counties. Nonetheless, I have no idea where I am going. I ask the dispatcher for directions, and she gives me some vague description of an unmarked road somewhere between here and Egypt. Worse yet, when I enter the address into the GPS, it is nowhere to be found. I'm going to have to wing it.

I cruise down Interstate 5 in The Green Reaper, the radio on low, emitting Christian rock, courtesy of the last investigator. Loose plastic dash molding clatters against metal. I could really use a new van. Uncharacteristically for December, the sun glares. I had forgotten my sunglasses, or rather I have no idea where they are. It is said that sunglass sales explode in the Pacific Northwest summer, because everyone has forgotten where they put their last pair before the great plunge into darkness and gloom that lasts from November through April.

I've written the address on the back of an envelope that this morning had contained a bill from the power company. The envelope rests on a coffee-stained clipboard and a ragged list of phone numbers for personnel no longer employed with us. I've got to get more organized.

The only thing I have figured out for sure by this point is where to turn off, though I haven't any idea whether I should turn right or left at the fork. On a whim, I turn left, and cruise towards, I hope, my destination. After about five minutes, I get worried and call the dispatcher back. She assures me that I'm on the right track, though she asks me for an ETA to the scene. I'm already about thirty minutes into this trip, and have God only knows how much farther to go.

I have no idea what my ETA is, so I randomly toss out a number: "Forty-five minutes." That should be enough time.

About an hour later, I see the signs for Darrington, and am relatively confident that my destination is approaching. As I sail past the tiny town and back onto the winding and lonely back roads, I realize that I am nowhere near the scene, and my ETA has been wildly inaccurate.

The dispatcher has relayed to me that Rounds Road should be somewhere between three mile markers, but once I pass the final one, I realize that I haven't passed anything resembling a road. Not one that is labeled as such, anyway. Back and forth I go along the same stretch, becoming more irritated as the minutes tick on.

I pull over and attempt to use the police radio on my dash. "Cascade from Union 301," I say.

Silence.

I look down at my phone. No bars. The only thing left to do is to continue to drive in one direction or another until I get either radio or cell reception.

I drive east, nearly to Egypt, I suspect, and wait for at least three bars to pop up on my screen before I call the dispatcher again. She tells me I've gone way past the increasingly mythical Rounds Road, but she'll have the deputy drive to the main highway to meet me. That would have been a fine idea in the first place.

Heading back west again, as short on fuel as I am on patience, I spot the familiar sight of a four-wheel drive pickup bearing the Skagit County Sheriff logo on the side. At last.

The stern expression on Deputy Campbell's face as he exits his truck indicates to me that he is not in the least amused by my directional misadventure. As I roll down my window to speak with him, I notice that no road sign exists, not even a hand-carved one, to give me an indication of the location of Rounds Road.

"I must have passed by this road three times," I say.

"Hmmm," he says, and launches into a brief synopsis of the circumstances. "Elderly guy found by his neighbor. Last seen yesterday afternoon when the neighbor came over to help him fire up his generator. Lock your hubs. It's rough going up there."

Deputy Campbell gets back in his truck, turns it around, and heads up an incredibly steep, narrow, rock-strewn, pothole-ridden road. I follow in my front-wheel drive van and hope for the best. After a nail-biting ten minutes, I arrive at a rustic log cabin in the woods. Had this been winter and there was snow on the ground, it would have been impossible to make it up here.

I get out of the van, hang my camera around my neck, grab my clipboard, and walk to the open front door of the cabin, where I am met by an older man with tears in his eyes. I introduce myself, offer condolences, and ask the usual questions: How long had he known Mr. Rounds? Did Mr. Rounds seem to be in his usual state of health when he was seen yesterday? Did he have any family?

Stepping onto the porch of the cabin, I feel like I am stepping back into the nineteenth century. A handmade canoe hangs just to the left of the open screen door. Various ropes and vintage logging tools hang to the right, along with a huge and rusty two-man saw. Deputy Campbell leads the way into the dark, musty-smelling home.

"Interesting story," says Deputy Campbell. "This guy was a mule packer. Everybody knew him around here. He and his wife were very well respected."

Pelts and antlers hang from the walls. The appliances are ancient. An iron stove, which appears to be the cabin's sole heat source, hulks in the corner. Tables overflow with yellowed documents, covered with dust. Pictures depicting a smiling older couple gaze out from the walls.

The dead man himself is not so easily identified, owing to the general clutter of the main living area. An upended walker lies in front of a dusty tube television, and beside that lies a thin man, facedown, his face obscured by a coffee table. I photograph as I approach. An empty liter bottle of vodka lies at the man's stocking-clad feet, next to a recliner, its fabric shiny with the sheen of years of body oils. Beneath the body are several firearms, including a rifle and a holstered revolver. I need to check to make sure the body is free of gunshot wounds.

I turn over poor old Mr. Rounds and he emits a guttural groan, as the last bit of air escapes his lungs. His face is purple, the eyes tightly closed, thick gray stubble on his chin. His hair is greasy and unwashed. I palpate the back of his skull and find a small defect. He's got a small laceration to the back of his head that roughly corresponds to the shape of the coffee table leg. There is no blood on the soiled carpet and no blood surrounds the room—a postmortem wound, sustained after his heart stopped, he collapsed, and his head struck the table. If the wound had occurred prior to death, or it had been the proximate cause of death, there would have been a great deal of blood. Likely it was a natural event that killed him.

The man's legs are swollen, reddened, and swaddled in soiled bandages. He wears a pair of dingy underwear and a stained T-shirt. His atrophied limbs exhibit the stiffness of fully advanced rigor mortis and the purple discoloration to his head and chest doesn't blanch with pressure. He has been dead about twelve hours.

I search the bathroom for medications and find only antibiotics prescribed to a long-deceased dog. Mr. Rounds, the neighbor tells me, didn't believe in doctors and visited only rarely. Looks like I will need to sign the death certificate.

A search of the kitchen, bedroom, and living area reveals no clue as to next of kin.

The neighbor wanders into the house again. "This wasn't him," he says, through tears. "He was a proud man. He wouldn't have wanted you to see him like this."

The neighbor provides me with a phone number for the executor of Mr. Rounds' estate, as well as some accompanying paperwork. He looks wistful. "After Chuck's wife died, he took to drinking. We couldn't get him to take a bath, but we just let him be."

I go back to the van and return with the gurney and plastic transfer sheet. The neighbor leaves the room and waits outside. "I don't want to see this part," he says.

Deputy Campbell and I ease Chuck onto the transfer sheet, onto the gurney, and into the van. I close the heavy metal doors and turn to face the neighbor.

"I'm gonna miss him," he says. "He was a good man."

I step into the van, start the engine, and begin to make my way down Mr. Rounds' eponymous road, past the trees he knew so well, on the way to the "big city" of Mount Vernon. It will take me over an hour to get the body to the morgue, but it is a peaceful trip, devoid of the pressure I felt responding to the scene.

The sun is going down, emblematic, I think, for the sunset of a life well lived, the first sun that will set in over seventy-eight years in a world without Chuck Rounds, mule packer, family man, fisherman, and homesteader. How often have I made this trip, taking the dead on their last earthly journeys? Bankers, teachers, lawyers, vagrants, drunks, and episcopal priests, all rendered quite similar in death.

It's a dismal way to make a living, I guess, but a privilege at the same time. How many others have the opportunity to see such a diversity of lifestyle, the personalities of the dead reflected in their surroundings, the way they've lived, and the ways they have died. Ostentation and pretense go by the wayside. The secret lives folks have lived, never letting anyone else in, are laid bare by death, sudden and often unexpected.

# Aria

She looks so much like my daughter. Both are nearing the conclusion of their first year on Earth, sprouting their first teeth, learning their first words, about to graduate from infancy to early toddlerhood. But my daughter, snoozing peacefully in her crib, is alive, and Aria is dead.

The ER nurse had a different tone to her voice than she usually did, laden with defeat and sadness. "We've got a one-year-old. Came in with CPR in progress." Terse and to the point, it was all I needed to know to be sure I would have to respond. All infant deaths are investigated, and all of them are autopsied.

My daughter, just learning to walk, had staggered to the baby gate, clung to its bars, and watched me descend the staircase to my van as she mumbled, "Dada, Dada, Dada."

The trip from my house to the Skagit County Hospital Emergency Department is short but seems more gravity-laden than most of my previous trips. This would be the first infant death I had investigated since the birth of my daughter, and I am uncertain how I will react in what is, effectively, a completely different mind-set than before. And then there are the more mundane thoughts, the practicalities. "Do I have an infant-sized body bag with me?" (Yes, sadly, they do make those, about the size of a pillowcase.) "Have I got the Infant Death Investigation Form with me? Is the battery in my camera charged? Do I have the Infant Re-enactment Kit with me?" The Re-enactment Kit consists of nothing more than a vaguely humanoid cloth doll that a mother would use to demonstrate the position in which she found her stricken baby.

It is good, I thought, that the doll had no face. Less to personalize the experience.

I arrive at the ER, packing my camera and clipboard full of forms. At the ER, the coroner is an unwelcome sight, especially when a baby has died. A Grim Reaper in cargo pants, I am the person nobody wants to meet, but without whom nobody can be buried.

The atmosphere is subdued among the ER staff, as it always is when a child has died. Even with sickness and injury surrounding doctors, nurses, and technicians every day, there is often levity, smiles, even downright jocularity. Not so when a baby has come in DOA. Medical people, so accustomed to seeing blood, hearing groans and wails on a regular basis, smelling feces and vomit, have developed a semi-permeable membrane to distance themselves emotionally from their work, allowing them to be compassionate but emotionally detached. No such membrane exists when it comes to children. Nobody ever gets used to children dying.

The ER clerk points to Room 5. The sliding glass door is shut and the curtains are drawn. A cart bearing coffee decanters is parked to the right, a sign that the staff are already attempting to minister to the survivors, offering a beverage, liquid solace, something warm to hold, a cup to grasp when one has no idea what else to do with their hands.

An uneasy feeling tugs at my gut as I slide open the glass door. I take a breath and push aside the curtain.

Neither parent glances up as I enter the room. The man has an arm wrapped protectively around his wife. Wrapped in a receiving blanket as though she were just born, her eyes wide open and staring vacantly at the ceiling, her face and tiny hands ashen and blue-tinged, is Baby Aria.

For several seconds, I am unable to speak. What does one say to parents who have just lost their daughter? My first few words come out as a stammer, but I manage to introduce myself and explain why I'm there, to investigate and hopefully find some answers in this terrible scenario. Briefly I consider telling the parents that my daughter is the same age, and that this will be difficult for me, but I think better of it. After all, my daughter isn't the one lying there dead just days before her first birthday.

"Tell me what happened today," I say.

The mother, still holding her dead daughter says, "I dropped her off at the babysitter this morning before work. She had a cough and a runny nose, so she had been fussy. The babysitter, Rosa, put her down for a nap about an hour before I came to pick her up. When I came to get Aria after work, I didn't want to disturb her nap, so I stayed and talked to Rosa for a while. She and I are friends, so we just made small talk. Then Rosa went upstairs to get Aria up from her nap and…"

The mother paused and took a long, sobbing breath. "And then, I heard screaming. Rosa said, 'Aria's not breathing!' and ran downstairs with her. She tried CPR until the medics got there."

The paramedics had scooped Aria's lifeless body into their arms and whisked her away to the ER, thumping on her small chest and attempting to breathe life into lungs that had probably been still for over an hour. Her back had shown the telltale purple discoloration of lividity, a clue that her blood had already begun to settle in the gravity-dependent parts of her body. It was more of a show for the parents, this frantic attempt to massage life back into the dead. Everyone knew she wasn't coming back.

The ER staff had continued the resuscitation efforts, Aria's mother watching the whole thing. Finally, there was nothing more left to do, and she was declared dead.

The initial run-down of the circumstances complete, it was now that dreaded moment when I had to take Aria from her mother.

"In need to examine and photograph her," I say. "It's best if you

128

step out for this part. Would you like to place Aria back on the bed?"

Silently and with the utmost of gentleness, Aria's mother tearfully places her dead daughter back on the hospital bed. She and her husband exit the room, leaving me with Aria.

The silence is deafening. It is almost as though her tiny presence fills the entire room with thick, heavy sorrow. I set to work.

I palpate her head to check for head wounds, depressions, any blood transferring to my gloves. Her hair is curly, clean, and fine, the hair of a baby. I look in Aria's eyes, checking for petechiae, the tiny hemorrhages that can indicate strangulation. I find none. Her eyes are beginning to cloud over, her pupils dilated and fixed. I check her mouth for any foreign objects or signs of injury, and then move to her trunk and limbs. She will need to be X-rayed in the morning, prior to autopsy, for any signs of new or old fractures, which might indicate abuse. So far, I find no outward signs of anything that could have caused Aria's death. I take the usual photographs, though she will be photographed again, in better detail, when she undergoes her autopsy tomorrow.

I close my camera case and place a blanket over Aria's still body, just to the chin. I then walk down the hallway to the chaplain's office to speak once again to the grieving parents and complete the dreaded Sudden Unexplained Infant Death Investigation form.

Since a baby's death is never a "normal" event, by any stretch of the imagination, a multi-page questionnaire has been developed in an effort to better elucidate the cause of an infant's untimely death. While it is excruciatingly detailed and leaves no stone unturned, so to speak, it is painful for both the grieving parents and, I suspect, every death investigator or detective who has to go through the process. It is intrusive, baring nearly every detail of the child's short life and every suspected shortcoming on the part of the parents. Questions range from "Was the child premature?" to "Has there been any recent painting or pest fumigating in the household?" Do the parents smoke? How many other

129

children live in the house?

Aria's mother answers all the questions, while her father remains in a teary daze, seemingly unable to even comprehend the events that have so recently transpired. Mount Vernon Police detectives are completing their own form in tandem, with the babysitter, and the forms will be compared later for consistency.

As I wrap up the interview, the mother asks, "What happens to her now?"

"She'll be taken…" I stumble on my words, "to the basement, where the morgue is located." The word "morgue" seemed so harsh, as did "basement." I could have chosen my words better.

Aria's mother looks hurt. "That's not what a mother wants to hear," she says, and I instantly flush with embarrassment.

There's nothing more to do now, than to speak to the detectives about their investigation, and begin the laborious process of writing up a report for the pathologist who will perform the autopsy in the morning.

My wife sends me a text message: "Are you okay?"

I text back "no."

I gather up my gear and head out the ER doors into the night, feeling the cold of December contrasting with the artificial atmosphere of the hospital. If one never looked out the window, it could be any season at all. The Green Reaper awaits.

Driving home, my only thought is of my own little daughter, sleeping peacefully in her crib. I couldn't imagine anything worse than losing her.

My wife is waiting up for me when I get home. She can see the toll this case has already taken on me.

"I need to see Klaire," I say. "I know she won't be happy with me when I wake her up, but I have to."

Klaire snoozes peacefully in her crib, in a position we call "stink-bug" with her rump in the air, her arms and legs curled underneath her, and her head to the side. She's wearing footed pajamas, a pink pacifier in her mouth. The room smells of lotion and baby wipes. Her sound machine glows blue in the corner of the room, emitting the sound of waves crashing to the shore. Moonlight shines through her blinds, illuminating the scant tufts of hair on her little head. She breathes. Thank God, she breathes.

Gently, I lift Klaire out of her crib and hold her to my chest. She whimpers. Her soft breath warms my cheek. I hold her for a few minutes, rock her, and thank God for her life.

I leave Klaire to her peaceful slumber, open up my laptop, and get to work. It's time to make sense of this tragedy, time to write the report.

It's a sleepless night.

# A Lonely Death

"So, this one's pretty bad," comes Sgt. Martinez's voice through the office phone. "The house is full of...all kinds of shit. She's been down at least a week or more."

"How old?" I ask.

"Born in sixty-six, so...forty-nine?"

Not even fifty. Definitely a call I need to respond to in order to rule out anything other than a natural death. What could have happened to her? Suicide, overdose, natural death, even homicide was a possibility. The inherent unpleasantness of examining a bloated, seeping corpse made missing a crucial detail, like a stab wound, much more possible. Extra vigilance was key.

I hang up the phone and go through my mental checklist of preparing to meet a decomposed corpse:

Heavy duty gloves: check.

Disaster Pouch: check. Love those things, but at $60 a pop, they aren't cheap.

Full body biohazard suit: check. The boss has been kind enough to leave one of those fully-encompassing outfits by the door, the sort that makes me look like Tinky Winky, from the Teletubbies. Stylish—no. Essential—most certainly.

I suit up in my Tinky Winky outfit prior to jumping into my county van, The Green Reaper. It's just a few blocks to the run-down trailer park where my client has been waiting for me, patiently, for days to weeks. It's still warm, late summer, and this fact makes for happy Northwesterners but unhappy undertakers. Warm weather and undiscovered bodies make for a dreadful combination.

I spot Sgt. Martinez's car, along with an unmarked detective vehicle, parked outside a nondescript, off-white mobile home. A beat officer and a detective stand outside the residence, which is never a good sign. I roll down the window to greet the officers. I can smell her from the street.

The odor of mammalian decomposition is like none other. Two ghastly chemical compounds, cadaverine and putrescine, combine to form a sickening olfactory signal that warns, "Stay away!" It seeps into any porous surface in a residence, be it a couch, curtains, clothing, or carpet. It clings to body hair, nasal hairs and mustaches, an unwanted hitchhiker that can linger for days.

Unfortunately for me, I've always been the sort who has run into situations that everyone else is running out of. Years ago, when I was a firefighter, I stretched hose lines into smoke-filled buildings as civilians coughed and headed for safety. These days, the danger is less, but the smell is worse.

"Ready?" says Detective Ford.

"As ready as I'll ever be," I reply.

I sling my camera around my neck, grab an extra set of gloves, and start towards the front door, the smell worsening with every foot I travel.

The yard is devoid of any landscaping whatsoever. Random weeds shoot up through the cracked and discolored concrete pathway that leads to a rotting front porch.

Once inside, it becomes obvious that my client was a very poor housekeeper. A dining-room table is heaped with a mountain of papers. Beer cans are strewn about the floor. A litter box in front of the table creates its own microenvironment of eye-watering stench. Brown fluid leaks from the refrigerator door. I open the door to a room that adjoins the kitchen. It is so full of beer cans the door cannot even be opened fully. Apparently this was her recycling room. In the bedroom is a stained mattress so covered with junk it seems that nobody would have been able to sleep there for some time.

"She had cats," says Detective Ford. "They all ran off into the neighborhood when we opened up the house."

There are no lights, so we have to work by flashlight. I catch a glimpse of a greenish-black lump on a couch in the living room, but resist the urge to immediately go over and photograph it. I have to document the scene before I move to the body.

"I found her purse stuck to the floor," says Detective Ford.

I examine it briefly before giving up. It smells strongly of rot and I decide to just bag it up and inventory the contents at the office. A key chain with multiple keys is attached.

Detective Ford picks up a seemingly empty cardboard beer container. "There's something in here," he says.

He shines his flashlight into it. "It looks like feathers, or...fur."

I take a look. The bottom of the box is full of what appears to be dark fur. Sitting atop the hairy mass are bones. I can identify a jaw and a few vertebrae. "Yup, it's a cat," I say. The poor thing looks like it's been there for a year or so. No flesh clings to the bones. It appears to have mummified before falling completely apart. I put the container back on the floor, unsure what to do with it.

Moving into the living room, I come face-to-face with the source of the terrible odor. Bloated terribly and wearing only a T-shirt, the woman reclines on her back, sinking into a dark couch made darker by inky dark green decompositional fluid that puddles on the floor beside her. Her skin is dark green amid islands of normal-appearing tissue. The Clostridial bacteria, freed from her intestinal tract upon her death, have infiltrated almost all of her tissue, blackening it and making the veins bulge. Maggots wriggle in her mouth, nose, and nether regions.

On the floor about her are multiple empty and half-empty cans of cheap beer, along with dozens of bright pink tablets scattered about the floor. Looking closer at her swollen, boggy face, I notice bright pink residue surrounding her lips and dribbling down her neck like badly applied cosmetics.

"I think that's Benadryl," says Detective Ford.

In combination with alcohol or even by itself in a high enough concentration, Benadryl can be deadly. Before I started with the Coroner's Office, I wasn't even aware it was possible to overdose on Benadryl, and I've seen two since then. Among other obscure overdoses I've seen are a fatal overdose on blood pressure medication and a death caused by the mistaken ingestion of laundry detergent. It seems people are always coming up with novel ways of removing themselves from circulation.

Dressed head to toe in a disposal, fluid-impervious suit and sporting a dual-canister filter mask, Officer Martinez makes his way into the dank and dark room to assist us with moving the woman's remains. It's an absurd scene, really. The guy closest to the body, the one poking, prodding, and inspecting, is the one who isn't wearing a mask. I guess one just gets used to the odor after a while—an olfactory overload of sorts.

After placing a sheet over the body to prevent squirting, splashing, or other untoward events, I heft her unceremoniously to the floor and into the waiting body bag. It's never a delicate process. We drag the bag into the living room and zip her up in a second, heavier bag to keep the smell down and the maggots from escaping and making a home in the back of my van.

After loading the body in my van, I thank the officers for their time and help, strip off my suit, and drive back to the office. I've got quite a lot of work ahead of me. Does she have any family? I've got no leads. Her mother had died months ago, and the prospect of searching through her belongings to find anyone who might survive her is unpalatable at best. I've got a report to write, a funeral home to contact, a purse to inventory, a death certificate to sign...All this, and I smell like a garbage truck.

I arrive at the morgue and slide the mortal remains of my client into the 42-degree "reefer." I hope she won't remain there more than three or four days, as the hospital employees on the upper floors complain if I keep a decomposed body there too long. I enter her name into the Book of Death, flick the lights off, and leave her in the company of another silent customer, an elderly man who had died from sepsis in the hospital.

Arriving at the office, I begin the odious task of inventorying the woman's purse, removing sticky gift cards, debit cards, scraps of useless paper, and the various and sundry detritus that accumulates in the abyss of a lady's handbag. Emptying each zippered compartment, I scribble down the contents on an inventory sheet.

After tallying the loose change and few crinkled bills, I arrive at one last exterior zippered compartment. It seems suspiciously full, as though the contents were not meant to be contained there. The zipper separates to reveal something unexpected...fur.

With gloved hands, I gingerly pull the object from its container. A kitten. So young its eyes had not yet opened, body slack with death, maggots darting under loosened skin and wiggling back out again.

I place the tiny animal on top of the soiled purse and snap a picture. Why, I'm not sure. Somehow I feel it's pertinent to the case. Did the woman place the kitten in her purse alive? Did it suffocate or was it already dead? Was this the final straw for the poor, lonely woman, the death of a kitten?

And then…the old familiar feeling washes over me again. That pressure that rises up from my chest and into my throat. The feeling of being overwhelmed, of having handed enough sorrow for one day. That feeling I have, so often times ignored, pushing on, faltering, at times raging at my family as I internalize and push deeper and deeper the things that I have seen.

Time for a break.

I want to give the kitten a proper burial but putting one foot in front of the other is all I can do at this point. I seal him (or her, I didn't look that closely) into a plastic sandwich bag and place him into the garbage can. I strip off my gloves and sink into a nearby chair for a minute. I've left the back door of the office open and the sunlight streams in, beckoning me.

Home is only five minutes away. I climb into the driver's seat of The Green Reaper and turn the key. The familiar stench of death emanates from the rear of the van, but I know I'm only minutes away from the rejuvenation that a hot shower brings.

At home, I put the Green Reaper in park. Thus commences the ritual detoxification. Once the garage door closes behind me, the layers begin to come off, first the boots, then the heavy Nomex pants and with them, the stink of death is peeled away. I climb the stairs into the house and unbutton my shirt. Off comes the belt and the badge. As I strip off the layers of clothing, a metaphorical weight comes off my shoulders. From a removalist to just another human being, tall, balding, and slightly paunchy. A father. A husband. A brother. A son.

The hot water cascades over me, cleansing me of the sadness and the loneliness, scrubbing clean the hairs on which cling the funk of decay. All I feel now is fatigue, and it's too early in the day for that.

I dry off, check my phone for messages, and open the sliding door to the outside world. The sun has always been a balm to me, its warmth searing away my worries, if only for a short while. The lawn chair awaits.

I sink into my chair and bask in the late summer sun. I put my headphones on and queue up some ELO. I'll get back to business in an hour or two, but now I'm just a middle-aged guy with a glass of iced tea in his hand, listening to the music of his youth, blissing out.

For a brief twenty minutes, I am left to my own little world, until my phone rings. Washington State Patrol requests the coroner. Traffic fatality on Highway 20. I put on a fresh uniform, slip on my dinged-up boots, and head to The Green Reaper. The mission continues.